Cross-Country Skiing and Snowshoeing

CROSS-COUNTRY SKIING AND SNOWSHOEING

BY

Erwin A. Bauer

Winchester Press

Second printing   1976

Copyright © 1975 by Erwin A. Bauer
All rights reserved

Library of Congress Catalog Card Number: 75–9255
ISBN: 0–87691–200–5

Library of Congress Cataloging in Publication Data

Bauer, Erwin A
    Cross-country skiing and snowshoeing.

    Bibliography: p. 205
    Includes index.
    1. Cross-country skiing. 2. Snowshoes and snowshoeing.
I. Title.
GV854.9.C7B38   796.9'3   75–9255
ISBN 0–87691–200–5

Published by Winchester Press
205 East 42nd Street, New York 10017

Printed in the United States of America

Contents

1 / The Quiet Revolution   11

2 / Origins and History   19

3 / Equipment   25

4 / The Well-Dressed Skier and Snowshoer   43

5 / Skis or Snowshoes?   55

6 / Ski-Touring Techniques   65

7 / Cross-Country Trails and Travel   77

8 / Camping and Overnighting   89

9 / Wildlife Watching and Photography   103

10 / Fishing and Hunting   115

11 / Coping with Common Winter Emergencies   129

12 / Avalanche!   141

13 / Where to Go: United States   149
     (compiled by Peggy Bauer)

14 / Where to Go: Canada   197
     (compiled by Peggy Bauer)

     Bibliography   205

     Index   209

To Peggy, who looks better breaking a trail than any other cross-country skier anywhere.

Cross-Country Skiing and Snowshoeing

1

The Quiet Revolution

ON AN INDELIBLE AFTERNOON toward the tag end of last winter, my wife, Peggy, and I drove from home, on the fringe of Grand Teton National Park, to where a plowed road suddenly dead-ended at the White Grass Ranch. That was ten miles or so away, and in the summertime we might have met a good bit of tourist traffic, especially around the Park visitor center at Moose. But after leaving US 187, the Yellowstone Road, we did not encounter another traveler.

Since the last storm, a snowplow had carved out a space big enough near the ranch to accommodate several cars. In that sheltered canyon among deep packed drifts, we parked and clamped thin, light wooden skis onto shoes with special toe bindings. We also donned rucksacks which contained survival items, cameras, and chocolates. Then we pushed up a steady, gentle slope toward the White Grass Ranger Station, closed since last October, and beyond it however far we decided to venture that day.

It was not one of those blinding bright afternoons one sees in travel posters of Jackson Hole. On the contrary, it was dark and threatening. Flurries of snow drifted sullenly downward, adding to the heavy load already clinging to evergreens along the thin trail. It was also cold, at least until we had skied far enough to warm our bodies up to "traveling temperature." Peggy guessed it was 20 degrees and maybe falling. But what I will remember most and longest about that day was the total quiet. Only the soft

During the dead of winter moose and other wildlife pay little attention to human approach.

hiss of skis on new snow broke the stillness. And around every turn in that wilderness trail was another scene of pure and lonely beauty.

A half mile from our starting point, heavy tracks meandered across the path ahead, and of course we stopped to see what made them. Looking back at us from the right, thin neck and back snow-sprinkled, was a moose. Black and brooding, it stared at us for a moment, as if doing a double take, then made no sound whatever as it turned and evaporated into the gloom. As easily as that, an animal that weighed nearly a thousand pounds had disappeared.

Now snow was falling more heavily, obliterating what would have been telltale tracks of the ruffed grouse we found some distance beyond the moose. But we spotted the grouse anyway. Most of the time this bird will flush—no, explode—so noisily as to unsettle a hunter. But when it spotted us, this one merely ran a few steps before takeoff, flying a short distance to a snowy tree perch in silence. How many times have you seen this species behave that way?

From the Ranger Station, which was only a snow-covered hump in a forest opening, the trail grew progressively steeper. At first it wound through park-like quaking aspens where, a few months before, we had photographed four bull elk bugling and challenging one another. Now in places we had to cut our own trail. But that was well worthwhile because in time we emerged atop a rim overlooking Phelps Lake. There, we enjoyed the magnificent view that thrills hundreds of hikers and backpackers every summer—

only we had the view all to ourselves, filtered through a brief break in the snowfall. Starting back down the trail, we looked for the Park Service sign which reads "Elevation 7500 Feet," but couldn't find it. It was buried somewhere well beneath us.

Now, for the first time, the quiet was occasionally broken. Scooting around bends and gaining speed downhill, Peggy was overcome by the thrill. She squealed and she laughed, and although muffled in the distance, it was wonderful. The last I heard before we reached the car—or rather before she reached it well ahead of me—was "bull moose here I co-o-oome!" From the fresh tracks I could tell that the startled beast was well on its way to Idaho by the time I got there. Peggy had already poured two cups of steaming beef broth.

Except for details about time and place, that afternoon was typical of countless others we have savored during recent winters. Some have been spent even closer to home—to the Lazy B—and in fact many began right at the front door, where skis are kept handy all season long. Other days we have wandered much farther. Our exploring begins in November, as soon as enough snow covers the ground to make it practical, and the skiing lasts as late as early April. In between, we seldom miss a day getting out, if only for a few hours. But no matter when or where, it is always the highest adventure.

Not all of our winter travel is on cross-country skis. Sometimes we go on snowshoes because under certain conditions these are much better. But the two together can convert an otherwise drab and dreary winter—some call it the "off season"—into the most exciting time of the year. For Peggy and me, skis and snowshoes have begun a new, exciting, and productive experience, a new way of life in winter.

I am a freelance outdoor, adventure, travel, and environment writer/photographer who several years ago made a move, too long delayed, from headquarters in the East to the Rocky Mountains, where both material and opportunities are much more numerous. But we quickly found that the deep snows of winter made some complications; on foot alone, we couldn't get around very far from the roads. One lucky day, which I will describe later, Peggy and I found it impossible to go fishing in the Snake River which remains largely ice-free throughout the winter. So we bought snowshoes to solve that problem. And shortly thereafter, Peggy and I ex-

For snowshoers in Jackson Hole, the awesome Tetons loom majestically in the background. This is the life, my friends.

changed pairs of skis for Christmas. In a whole career of acquiring far more outdoor gear than any one family requires, the cross-country skis and snowshoes have been by far the best bargains ever. For a total outlay of less than $300, we have bought several winters of undiluted pleasure and adventure almost beyond describing. No rifle or shotgun, no flyrod or new car ever gave greater rewards.

First let's make it clear that we are not speaking of downhill or Alpine skis or skiing. Nor is this book about the kind of skiing that takes a person to America's popular ski slopes, where crowds are the rule and standing in line at ski lifts takes up too much time, where parking lots are quick to fill up and wallets are just as quick to empty. Instead I'm writing about cross-country or Nordic or ski-touring skis which anyone of modest strength and coordination can use almost as easily as snowshoes, or hiking boots. This volume will be about the quiet world, as far as possible from the busy slopes and especially from the snowmobilers, a world that anyone, regardless of age or sex or income, can relish.

Cross-country skiing and snowshoeing alone, with no particular goal in mind, are fun and rewarding. Aside from being activities that bring a person into the fresh outdoors, both are excellent physical conditioners during a period that might (normally?) be inactive. A skier or snowshoer can be as vigorous or as leisurely as he likes; he can set his own pace. Here is an activity which brings many different muscles into play. It is an exercise as healthful as it is enjoyable. Moreover, it is an escape from the ordinary.

Here also is a means to other ends—to fishing, hunting, trapping, bird or wildlife watching, photography, exploring places that might be inaccessible at other seasons. We've done all of these and more. We have also revisited familiar summertime haunts, only to find that in the grip of winter they are even more beautiful. We have visited in comfort the same places where clouds of mosquitoes descended on any interloper during July and made the place miserable. We have also discovered new nooks and hideaways we never knew existed before.

Cross-country skiing can be done whenever and wherever enough snow—usually just a few inches—falls to cover the ground— and that includes a good portion of North America. In northern latitudes the snow cover might accumulate to several feet and remain for a very long time. At such times there is no other way to get around on foot.

A cross-country skier or snowshoer doesn't need any special or costly facilities such as lifts or trams, graders, and snowplows to clear away an arena or runway. Crowded and noisy lodges or chalets are not part of the picture. Feet are not encased in heavy plastic anchor weights. And a Nordic skier or snowshoer requires no elegant, color-coordinated, imported-from-Austria wardrobe to sustain status among other skiers. Instead he dresses for comfort, wearing clothes that will keep him dry and warm.

Cross-country travel is not a sport or activity conceived of artificiality, snob appeal, and high-octane promotion; rather it depends on the silence and magic of the outdoors. It's a quiet revolution.

Snowshoes can take you to places where your only company will be a hillside of snowy ghosts.

Youngsters take readily and easily to the quiet world. Cross-country skiing is even easier than learning how to walk.

This revolution is one which all can join. Go for a few hours, a weekend or a week. Depending on your mood, you strike out alone or travel with a congenial group. Or make it a family affair. We've met members of three generations out together and no gaps were noticeable. We've also seen youngsters hardly old enough to walk doing very well on skis, in fact on the very same shafts that big sister used in learning to break snow a couple of years before.

Speaking of economy, there is an annual church basement bazaar each November in our town where parents can swap smaller skis for progressively larger ones as their broods grow up. And far out on the trails we've met many of the same grandmothers who serve the oatmeal cookies and coffee at the bazaar. You can ski and snowshoe as long as you can shuffle one foot ahead of the other. Unlike in downhill skiing, there is virtually no danger of broken bones or serious injury of any kind. You don't pitch headlong into eternity, but you do pass slowly enough to enjoy the white world all around.

Near the end of one glorious day last March, Peggy and I crossed a wide-open meadow homeward bound as we had many times before. Because spring wasn't far away and a warm sun had melted a thin layer of surface snow, our skis swooshed louder than usual and, biting deep, our ski poles crunched in even cadence. But when we stopped to rest we could detect no other sound except the soft gurgle of a recently thawed stream flowing unseen beneath the snow. Not even the pair of Canada jays that glided to a perch nearby, hoping to freeload tidbits, made any sound at all. Total peace and quiet.

"In another two months," Peggy reminded, "this place will be something else."

It would indeed. Thousands of tourists would stop in almost that same spot where an asphalt turnout was not now visible. Most would pause only long enough, I realized, to snap the scene of majestic mountains and a meadow in the foreground carpeted with lupine and arrowleaf balsamroot. Then they would race onward to somewhere else in air-conditioned cars or motorhomes. They were missing a lot, I mused to Peggy, tearing around like that.

Surely the time has come to slow down—to park the plush autos, to get out of the jets, and make some honest footprints of our own. It's for our own well-being. In winter we can do it with skis or snowshoes and have the time of our lives. We can join the quiet revolution, which happens to be quiet (and peaceful, too) in more ways than just one.

THE SNOW-SHOE DANCE.

TO THANK THE GREAT SPIRIT FOR THE FIRST APPEARANCE OF SNOW.

2

Origins and History

AMONG THE COUNTLESS, now nostalgic scenes published a century ago by those pioneer printmakers to the American people, Currier and Ives, is the fanciful one shown at left, "The Snow-Shoe Dance." The subtitle to the print reads "to thank the great spirit for the first appearance of snow." As you can see, the redskins, though wearing feathered headdresses, are bare to the waist. Just why they would welcome a snowfall when so scantily attired is hard to explain; perhaps it's just the eastern Indian's answer to the western rain dance.

In any case, the print is significant because, with very few other exceptions in the history of American art, this is the earliest illustration of any devices being used for cross-snow travel on foot. That is a strange thing, because snowshoes are at least 60 centuries old. For thousands of years the invention of the snowshoe remained as important as the invention of the wheel, because it permitted people to travel—no, actually to survive and prosper—in the northern regions of the earth where wheels were useless. No one really knows who made or used the first snowshoes, or exactly where the deed was done. But we're fairly certain that one such device for easier transport over snow was used 4000 years B.C. in Mongolia.

Even more obscured in northern thaw mists and time is the origin of skis. It is certain that skis were used since the beginning of recorded history in Scandinavia and that the very word is derived from the old Norse *skith*. Like snowshoes, the first known skis were really slats or shingles of any shape which mostly extended the foot (giving it a greater sole area and therefore better purchase to stay on top of the snow) rather than the long smooth runners we know today. Evolution from the old ski to the present was slow and is still going on.

If we can assume that Asia and North America were once connected rather than separated by the Bering Sea, other facts fall more easily in place. A land bridge here explains how the Indians and Eskimoes reached this continent by migration from central Asia. It also explains how the use of snowshoes by indigenous peoples was prevalent all over Canada and the United States when the first European visitors arrived, and remained so until the late 19th century when Scandinavians began to arrive in numbers in the New World.

However, there are mysteries that need solving. For example, the Norse wanderer, Leif Ericson (who arrived in North America about five centuries before the Pilgrims waded ashore at Plymouth Rock), made no mention at all of cross-snow devices being used. His accounts were otherwise very detailed. Why not? On the other hand, we know that Indians were by far the most dependent on snowshoes and were greater innovators than the Eskimoes. But why? However, there may be partial explanation for that. Eskimoes did not have available, for one thing, the materials to make snowshoe frames.

Living farther south, Indians (who had wood aplenty) had to travel through generally softer snow conditions below the world's treeline. Of necessity they wore some kind of foot extenders through the winter of the year or remained immobile. Starvation was the alternative. Eskimoes, on the other hand, traveled more where the annual snowfall averaged less (that's true) and where that snow may have been packed more solid by ceaseless Arctic winds—or they traveled on rock-hard ice floes. Still there was a critical period late every springtime when rapid snow melting restricted Eskimoes to a thin strip along coastlines and prevented any hunting inland. That was their hunger moon.

Thanks mostly to the pioneer Indian artist George Catlin, we know that at least some Plains Indians occasionally used snowshoes to hunt buffalo. During severe winters, the great beasts, weighing a ton or more, couldn't possibly stay atop the snow. But Sioux and Blackfoot braves on webbed snowshoes could. They could therefore approach to within point blank bow and arrow or even spear range to obtain a supply of fresh meat and a warm robe all at the same time.

But it was the Athapascan Indians (of the North American West) and the Algonquins (of the Northeast) who most relied on snowshoes. They therefore made better ones and greatly improved the designs. Beginning with a basic pattern which was roughly egg-shaped and called (at least today) the bearpaw, each group produced shoes best suited to their own particular conditions of geography, of quality and quantity of snowfall. Some tribes used different shoes from season to season. On snowshoes fashioned skillfully out of the materials readily at hand—green saplings and the thong of deer, moose, or caribou—an Algonquin or Athapascan Indian was even more mobile in winter than he might have been in the mosquito-infested, lush underbrush of summer.

The main change in snowshoes from the oldest known museum artifact to present factory-made pairs has mostly been in improved craftsmanship, in gradually altered wooden-frame and rawhide-web designs. Two exceptions are worth noting. From time to time Indians of Labrador (and, more than likely, elsewhere) made shoes of all wood. These were split or hewn boards, preferably of spruce, although pine and basswood would do. The shape was oval, or bearpaw, and with the availability of metal tools (after Europeans arrived) the shoes were easier to make than webbed shoes. The other exception is the recent use of aluminum tubing for frames and vinyl webbing, an improvement that was almost inevitable in a technological age. More on these in the next chapter.

Of all the Europeans who began the settlement and colonization of eastern North America, the French most quickly accepted and appreciated Indian ways. Not that they were any more adaptable than the English, say, or the Dutch, but they happened to be located farther north, in country where canoes and especially snowshoes came in handier. This gave them considerable advantage during that prolonged guerilla fighting for control of eastern North America—in what we know as the French and Indian War.

Most history books still refer to a certain 1758 engagement in the Adirondacks near Lake George as the Battle of Snowshoes. It may not have been very decisive, but it taught all contestants the value of being able to get around quickly over deep snow cover. Soon snowshoes were issued as basic equipment to fighting men, both in the British armies and in the various state (colony) militias.

Snowshoes were used by restless scouts, explorers, woodsmen, and especially by trappers during the gradual opening of the American West to a far greater extent than is generally realized. In many places winter survival depended entirely on them. Among the relics saved by oldest pioneer ranchers here in Jackson Hole are a few now-brittle old snowshoes used by their grandparents. These might have been bought from Indians or have been "homemade" of sudden necessity. Now and then, when the drifts pile up too deep for horses and the family snowmobile breaks down, even today's rancher will have to fall back on snowshoes (or skis) to feed livestock in an emergency. Throughout the winter webs are standard equipment in the four-wheel-drive pickups of game wardens in Wyoming and elsewhere in the snow belt.

For a long time during the past century, particularly around the cities of Eastern Canada, snowshoeing clubs were popular, prestigious, and all the rage. Regular outings were held, and expeditions planned for members. Clubs had distinctive insignia, elegant uniforms, mascots, even bands and drill teams. But recently the interest and enthusiasm for snowshoeing has taken other directions, as we shall see. It is today a less gregarious, more quiet and contemplative sport. Few of today's most serious snowshoers could also be classified as joiners, except perhaps in the Sierra Club or Wilderness Society.

Today many modern armies maintain elite organizations of ski troops. Ski soldiers could play important parts in future conflicts over the precious natural resources being discovered at the polar ends of the earth. Cross-country ski events are now part of the World Olympics and one event, the biathlon, combines skills at both skiing and shooting.

At least to Americans, the history of skiing lacks the color and interest of snowshoeing history, because it is newer. Even though, as mentioned earlier, Scandinavian immigrants introduced skiing, the sport never really caught on until the 1930s. Since then its popularity has been extraordinary; no corner of snow country in North America is without its ski resorts and slopes. Whole new industries, economies, and lifestyles have been created around skiing.

Still, until recently this boom concerned only downhill or Alpine skiing, not the kind where a person propels himself across the quiet, white countryside. It is indeed true that a small hard core of cross-country skiers was keeping the greatest winter pastime to themselves, especially in New England. But it wasn't really until the mid-1960s—the same time that so many Americans suddenly realized it was time to turn a corner in our headlong, artificial rush to nowhere—that cross-country skiing finally caught on everywhere from the low Poconos and Berkshires to the High Sierra.

So there it is: a sport with little color and even less tradition, with few records to break or impressive statistics to compile. Unlike football and baseball, the circus sports, which thrive on crowds, hysteria, hero worship, and halls of fame, here is a purist sport that has everything.

Great personal achievement and satisfaction. Physical well-being. Escape. Quiet. You simply can't match that combination. As Teddy Roosevelt emphasized so well: "It is better to do something yourself, and do it poorly, than watch somebody else do something well." The best response to that is "Amen!"

3

Equipment

THE MOST SIGNIFICANT SINGLE FACTOR about ski-touring or snow-shoeing is that only a small amount of equipment is necessary to enjoy—even to excel at—either or both. Cross-country gear is comparatively inexpensive and perhaps the best bargain in all sports equipment. Given proper care, it can last for many seasons, some of it for a lifetime of winters spent outdoors.

Let's consider skiing first. The participant will need the following basic items: skis, boots, poles, waxing kit, and either a light rucksack or waist carrier for spare items. We'll discuss proper clothing in the next chapter.

The main difference between downhill and cross-country skis is in the boot fastening. For downhill skiing the entire boot is firmly affixed only at the toe. This difference is what makes possible the combination jogging-skating that takes you, uphill and down, smoothly over the landscape.

The earliest cross-country skis were nothing more than solid slivers split from hardwood tree trunks. As recently as 1973–74, however, over eighty percent of all skis sold were of sleek, tough, laminated wood, most with lignostone (compressed beech) edges. But suddenly that is changing. New and even tougher skis of fiberglass captured a much greater part of the market beginning in 1974 and almost certainly will be the dominant skis in years to come. In the past, synthetics have been more expensive than wooden skis. But as hickory, the best wood, becomes prohibitively

Basic cross-country gear: light wooden skis, standard toe bindings to fit ski boots, ski poles, waxing kit with various waxes, scraper, cork to spread wax.

Here—in one photo—is illustrated the difference between downhill and cross-country skiing. In cross-country, the boot is affixed only at the toe, to permit easy jog-gliding over the snow.

expensive (Its only source is in the U.S., while most leading ski makers are in Europe.), nearly all cross-country skis of the future will likely be of fiberglass or some other synthetic.

Years ago when writing on fishing books, I was confronted by the subject of rods, rod actions, and the inevitable which-rod-is-best-for-which-fishing controversy. I collected all the research material available, obtained and tested countless rods. But it remained something I never really mastered or understood. And if anyone ever did, it seemed, he would be too exhausted to have any fun fishing.

So it also seems to be with cross-country skis, about which a bewildering amount of bewildering material has been written. Pick up any manual or manufacturer's catalog and you read about "tip-follow characteristics," "poor kick glide," "stress cycles," "lateral flexes," and "air-channel cores"—all this non-language, until you may conclude that ski-touring is either impossible or not worth the effort. It reminds me of how, not long ago, many angling writers tried to make fly-fishing appear complicated and preposterous rather than the simple, pleasant sport it is. Another parallel is provided by the photographer who knows everything about cameras and lenses except how to take pictures.

So it has been with cross-country skis. Without a doubt, some addicts, genuine experts—perhaps racers or other competitors—can revel in the complexity and nitpicking of ski selection. But the truth is that almost anyone can put on any good pair of skis today and have fun getting across country better than ever before. Sure, skis should be of proper length and weight to match the skier's physique, and to that end we've provided a guide table of ski (and pole) lengths. The skier should also consider how often, and where, and under what kind of conditions he will most often be skiing. Let's go from there.

As a rule of thumb, the proper ski length is determined as follows. Stand flat on the floor, feet together, and extend one hand almost straight overhead. The ski length should equal the distance from floor to palm of hand. With time and experience, a skier may discover that slightly longer or shorter skis are better.

For purposes of simplicity here, consider that there are three types of Nordic skis: Call these *touring*, *light-touring*, and *racing*. They differ in width, weight, the type of bindings, and the boots which are worn with them.

Most skis today are in the touring category, although with increased skill, there may be a growing preference toward light-touring outfits. Touring skis weigh six to seven pounds a pair and are 55 to 65 millimeters wide. (In all catalogs and most references

Ski/Pole Length Guide

	Height Ft.	In.	Ski Length (cm.)	Pole Length (cm.)
Men	5	1	195	120
	5	3	200	125
	5	5	205	130
	5	7	210	135
	5	9	210	140
	5	11	210	145
	6	1	215	150
	6	3	220	155
Women	4	9	185	110
	4	11	185	115
	5	1	190	120
	5	3	190	125
	5	5	195	130
	5	7	200	135
	5	9	205	140
Children	3	4	120	—
	3	7	130	—
	3	9	140	—
	4	0	150	90
	4	2	160	95
	4	5	170	100
	4	7	180	105
	4	9	185	105
	4	11	190	110
	5	1	195	115
	5	4	195	120
	5	6	200	125

Proper ski length is approximately equal to the height you can reach with outstretched hand.

the dimensions of cross-country skis are given in the metric system.) These are the best skis for most beginners with modest coordination (who may have balance problems) and/or who will not ever spend a great deal of time using them. However, they are also the choice of most wilderness skiers, of winter backpackers and mountaineers, and of anyone toting a heavy load. The boots to use with these are cut above the ankle, like hiking boots. The bindings are steel or aluminum alloy toe pieces, some with heel cables or straps.

Light-touring skis give slightly less support and stability than touring skis. But for persons of good coordination and balance, traveling without packs or in fairly even country, light-touring skis are faster and to be preferred. The skis weigh about four pounds and measure 48 to 53 millimeters wide. The boots are cut at the ankle and bound with aluminum alloy toe clamps.

Racing skis, the lightest, may weigh less than three pounds and measure less than 50 millimeters. Low-cut boots similar to track shoes fit onto skis with lightweight aluminum toe clamps. They are for racers and very experienced, athletic skiers only.

For the best performance on almost every kind of ski, it is necessary to wax the bottoms, and there are different waxes for different snow conditions. That means it may be necessary to wax, rewax, or change waxes daily, if not more often. Depending on your temperament, waxing can be a nuisance and maybe even a major headache. If so, consider a wood-base ski which works well with little wax and at times none at all. And at least check out the other skis with "fish scale," mohair strips, and similar undersurfaces which never require wax. Most accomplished skiers and equipment sales people scoff at these, but some no-wax skis are not all that bad. If you don't mind the chore of waxing, however, composition wood, plastic, and/or fiberglass bases are by far the best for you.

Of course snow conditions vary greatly across the country and throughout the season. Now think for a moment about the most typical, frequent conditions where *you* ski. If the snow is normally soft, you need no special hard edges on the skis. But the harder the snowpack, the more important it is to have hard lignostone or aluminum edges. That is doubly true in steeper country where downhill runs call for greater control.

So select a complete category—touring, light-touring, or racing—with the skis matched to suit your size, physique, and snow situation. If you are just beginning in this game and naturally have doubts about selection, ask your dealer if you can try out different outfits before finally buying one. In many communities the dealers also operate ski equipment rentals where it is easy to try out a wide range of skis, and where you are given the credit of the rental against buying a new pair. I strongly advise this course as the way to locate gear that fits and feels best on your own two feet. It beats all the reading you can do, including this book.

Ski boots are available in leather and synthetics, with leather and synthetic soles, lined (with fur or synthetic pile) and unlined, below and above the ankle lengths. All synthetic boots should be lined (except for racing) because this material is a poor insulator. Keep in mind that although synthetics are waterproof, they cannot be repaired as can leathers. Which boot to buy is again a matter of personal preference, and again there is wisdom in trying before buying, if possible.

Good inexpensive gear is available for youngsters, and it can be traded in after every season for larger skis, as the kids grow up.

You'll be comfortable with a ski pole that reaches a height equal to just underneath your upper arm.

Any boots should fit snugly, well, but not really tight. At least that is my own preference. I like to have a little extra room in the toe. When trying on boots, do so with the same socks (or at least exactly the same sock thickness) you will wear when skiing.

There are in existence some bindings that permit cross-country skis to be used with any hunting or hiking boots or pacs. They work well enough in a pinch, but balance suffers compared to special ski-touring boot bindings, and so are mostly unsatisfactory. Don't skimp and try to get by with them.

The handiest bindings are the three-peg types, usually installed free on the skis in the shop where you buy them. These clamp onto the boots by thumb pressure or pushing down with the point of the ski-pole tip. Some offer a slight adjustment for tighter clamping for wilderness or steep-country touring. The main thing is to be certain that, whatever the bindings, they do not twist off too easily at every sudden bend in a trail or sudden shift in balance.

The ideal binding is one which allows the same foot freedom and flexibility as when walking in the most comfortable, broken-in hiking shoes—or even in sneakers. Nowadays the squarish cut of all boot soles and bindings is the same and the dimensions between the triplet (always three) binding pegs have been standardized. This means that a skier can select any boots and any skis—and be assured the two will fit. Obviously they will also be interchangeable, even if the skis were made in Norway and the boots in Finland.

Two poles are necessary for cross-country skiing. The shafts come in metal, bamboo, and fiberglass. Most pros prefer the metal or glass, which are also more expensive. Stand flat, feet together and with one arm parallel to the floor; the proper pole length is measured from the floor to just underneath your upper arm. For racing, thin, whippy shafts are the ticket, but ski-tourers need something more substantial.

The softer the snow, the larger the diameter of the baskets at the bottoms of ski poles should be. In what might be called normal or average snow conditions, baskets of say 4½-inch diameter are fine. In wet snow or soft powder, 6-inch diameter is much better. Look for pole grips and loops (these should be adjustable) that fit your hands in all skiing positions. Keep in mind that you will probably wear only light gloves (or bare hands) during light, fast touring, but you will probably need mittens when normally tour-

Webbing and neoprene bindings are used with these aluminum-frame shoes. Notice the small size of snowshoe necessary to support a person on top of snow.

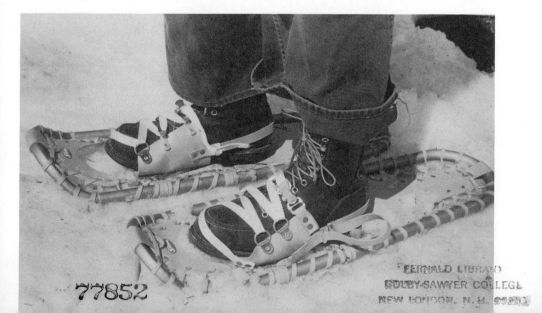

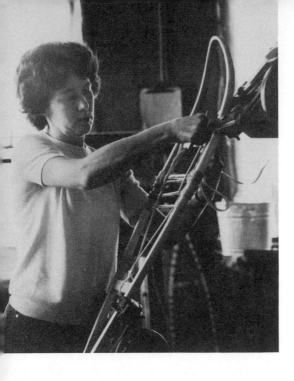

In the Tubbs plant at Wallingford, Vermont, a lady craftsman strings webbing on a wooden-frame snowshoe.

ing and exploring, particularly on colder days.

Not nearly as much bewilderment (or choice to a buyer) goes into a purchase of serviceable snowshoes. As pointed out previously, the basic design hasn't changed much in centuries. Today a person pays as much (or as little) for craftsmanship as he does for anything else. If there is anything really confusing about snowshoes, it is the nomenclature. For instance there are bearpaws, teardrops, trappers, Alaskans, guides, rangers, Adirondacks, crosscountrys, Michigans, Maines, Sherpas, and probably more others than we could ever list here. But depending on the manufacturer or place or origin, any two or three of these may be exactly the same or very nearly so.

However, no matter, because the well-known basic snowshoe design is that of an oval or elongate frame, crisscrossed, or actually loosely woven, with webbing. Traditionally the framing is of some kind of wood. Today the best wooden shoes are framed with New England white ash, which is straight grained, strong fibered and can be set to shape. Recently frames of aluminum tubing have entered the picture. Stiffness in the frame, any frame, is desirable.

All webbing today is made of rawhide thong or neoprene, a

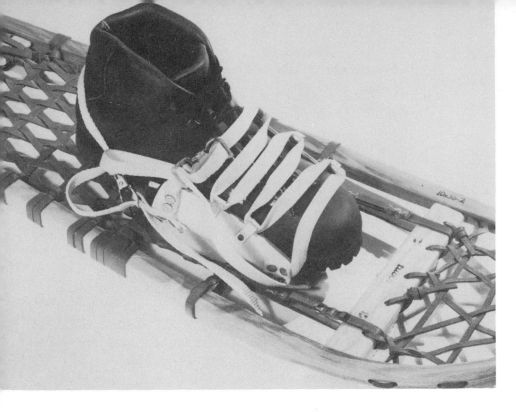

Binding straps of synthetic web belt this standard hiking boot to the snowshoe.

These wooden-frame shoes feature neoprene bindings. The snowshoer is using ski-touring boots and is wearing gaiters from knee to ankle.

synthetic. The latter may not be as aesthetically appealing as raw-hide, but it has a good many practical advantages. Neoprene is lighter than leather (which stretches) when wet, seems to resist wet snow build-up better, is impervious to petroleum products (too often snowshoes are stored over the summer in garages), and is rodent-proof. In the past, rats, mice, and porcupines, even family dogs, have accounted for as many snowshoe webs as hard use when traveling across country.

It has been claimed, but without total credibility, that short, broad shoes are best for woods and brush because they are easier to maneuver. On the other hand, longer, thinner shoes were considered best for going across the open. Webbing should also be "tighter," closer together for soft, fluffy snow conditions. But more than likely, personal preference should be the main factor. I find it easier to walk under any circumstances in the thinner shoes; other snowshoers I know are exactly opposite.

The main thing is to use a model or shape with sufficient surface to support a given weight—the snowshoer plus whatever load he carries—over the snow. This is to say that a heavier man needs a larger shoe/webbing surface underfoot than a frail man. It is uncomfortable and fatiguing to wear snowshoes that are too small because the wearer sinks in too far with each step. It is also a waste of energy for a small person to trudge along on shoes that are bigger than necessary. Fortunately, it isn't hard to pin down the proper size with accuracy.

One of the oldest and probably the biggest manufacturers of snowshoes is Tubbs of Wallingford, Vermont. The company has been doing business in the same stand for over 100 years, and their catalog (like most others) lists the exact size and capacity of each model shoe. That makes selection much easier.

Say you weigh 200 pounds or so and might at times lug a load of mink traps on your back. You live in Maine where snow tends to be soft and the second-growth woodlands are choked here and there with brush. You will also, most likely, have to cross frozen swamps and marshlands. The Green Mountain Bear Paw, which measures 10 inches wide by 36 inches long, advises Tubbs, is the best bet for you. It's the same shoe the wardens of the Vermont Fish & Game Department prefer.

A main feature of any snowshoe is the cross member forward

Turned-up ends on these shoes make the going easier in deep snow, and prevent snow from collecting on the tips.

Various sizes of Sherpa shoes. These are almost certainly the utilitarian snowshoes of the future.

of the balance center with an opening (no webbing) just in front of it. The snowshoe binding is such that the ball of the foot sits— pivots, really—right on top of this cross piece. When the snow- shoer walks, his toes dip down back and forth into the opening. As the foot is raised for a step forward, the binding attachment permits the tail of the snowshoe to drop down. And the toe flips upward. The number of different bindings developed to permit this action is even larger than the number of shapes of snowshoes. At least there are far too many to describe in detail here.

Your goal should be to find a binding that most firmly accom- modates your boot without permitting any side-to-side twist of the shoe. You may have to do some experimenting to achieve this. Incidentally, any kind of hunting or hiking boots can be used. I like insulated high tops (12 inches, say) with rubber bottoms to keep out snow. If your boots are lower than that, wear cross- country skiing gaiters over the boot tops. For more advice on boot selection see Chapter 4.

Some snowshoes have long tails; some do not. In the past, the tail probably served as a sort of rudder which, by dragging, helped keep the shoe pointed straight ahead. In other words, it com- pensated for the slack in loose (inefficient) binding attachments. But with good bindings these are mostly unnecessary and in fact only an extra weight to trudge around.

But back to bindings. The best are those which are easy to attach and buckle to the boot, a great feature when hands are numb with cold. The binding should freely hinge up and down to at least a 45-degree angle when the snowshoe is held up off the ground. There should be very little slack, or play, from side to side. The attachment should be secure enough that the boot does not work forward when going downhill, and it should not need frequent readjustment when traveling.

Some snowshoes are turned up at the tips, others are not, but in general a turned-up tip has advantages. Mostly it helps prevent the tip from digging into the snow every time the shoe is lifted to take a forward step. A straight or flat tip may collect snow, which even in small amounts adds to the labor of walking. Even- tually the wearer may feel that he is shoveling out a path ahead rather than walking on one. For me, anyway, a turned-up tip is well worth the slight extra cost (because the manufacturer must

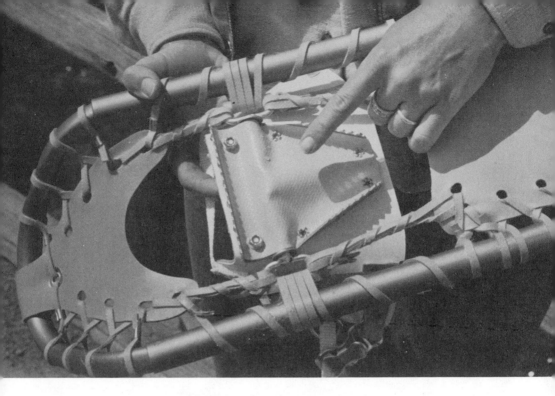

The unique bottom of Sherpa shoes makes for easier, safer climbing and better going on hard surfaces.

"work" the frame to that curved shape) and especially so when going downhill.

According to Sir John Hunt, who led the successful assault on Mt. Everest in 1953, a unit of weight on the foot is equal to five units carried on the back. Perhaps so, but the ratio might be even greater. Therefore the lighter your snowshoes, the less energy you will require to travel any distance comfortably. That is an extremely good reason for considering the new aluminum frame snowshoes developed and sold by Bill and Barbara Prater of Tacoma, Washington.

As pointed out earlier, the evolution of snowshoes from the very first ones known has been very slow. Changes have been few. But the Praters' radically new Sherpa snowshoes really do introduce something original and worthwhile for serious snowshoers. Besides the aluminum frames, a steel-plated hinge rod, with a nylon bushings for wear, is mounted right into the snowshoe. As mounted onto this rod, the bindings can be rotated freely up and down, but

For a total investment of less than $100 this novice skier has bought many years of fun and excitement.

without any slack from side to side. For the first time, according to the Praters, this makes for precision foot placement, for perfect tracking on the trail. Our own testing surely confirms that.

But there is still more to the Sherpa shoes. The underside of the binding has built-in traction in the form of serrated edges (aluminum teeth) to provide any-direction traction under the ball of the foot on hard crust snow or even on ice. Even the webbings are not traditional: In fact a neoprene "decking" (which looks like a miniature trampoline inside the frame) mostly replaces the criss-crossed rawhide thongs so that smaller and lighter shoes can be worn to support the same weight. Snow doesn't cling to the neoprene.

Actually the Sherpa snowshoes are maintenance-free for a long, long time. Here is probably the working snowshoe of the future, especially in the mountains.

Most snowshoers carry along one ski pole rather than the two of cross-country skiers because balance is more assured. The pole should have a large basket of six-inch diameter. Some prefer an ice axe with a basket attached to the point end as a walking aid. In rough and mountainous conditions, this is better than the ski pole.

Both skiers and snowshoers will want some kind of small carrier for survival and emergency items, for repair pieces, wax, lunch, film, and cameras. There is the choice between the waist or belt pack preferred by many skiers and a light, waterproof rucksack, the size depending exactly on how much you want to lug along. I prefer a compartmented day-use rucksack which can hold several lenses as well as the other items, simply because I never cut across country without cameras. Another possibility is a light pack-basket. And we have also met snowshoers who carry everything in several oversize pockets sewn into their clothing.

Because this chapter was written late in 1974, at a time when prices of all commodities were rapidly increasing, often doubling overnight, I've carefully avoided discussing costs. They can change too easily. But as a very rough guide, in November 1974 a serviceable and high-quality cross-country skiing outfit (skis, boots, bindings, poles, wax kit) could be bought for $100. Best-quality ash-framed snowshoes were going for $50 a pair. Aluminum frames with neoprene webs cost twice that much. Comparatively, though, any of these was a great investment in pure pleasure and high adventure.

4

The Well-Dressed Skier and Snowshoer

UNLIKE PARTICIPANTS in so many sports, the cross-country skier and snowshoer is absolutely free of fashion dictates and restraints. There is no "color for this season," no "trends" or "looks." If the clothing worn accomplishes only two ends, it is acceptable. These two purposes are first, keeping warm and dry and second, allowing maximum movement. The damp snowshoer will inevitably become chilled and the skier who can't squat or move his arms easily is in for discomfort and early fatigue. But while nothing in particular is required, there are general pieces of clothing needed to make the sport enjoyable which, after all, is the whole point.

The principle of layers in clothing was never more important than it is to the ski-tourer or snowshoer. In discussing these it's most logical to begin with the first and work outward. So let's start with underwear. For comparatively mild weather, you may need only everyday combinations constructed of cotton. Nylon and other man-made fibers are not recommended; they frequently do not bend or give as much as cotton and they are never absorbent.

When the temperature is lower and/or the wind velocity higher, more protection is needed. You then think in terms of long underwear. The two-piece variety will work well; fishnet is a favorite, and lightweight thermal is also good. If you wear knickers you might consider cutting off a pair of bottoms to just above the knees. That amount of warmth should be right for average conditions.

For snowshoeing or skiing when the thermometer threatens to bottom-out and the wind waves the tips of the evergreens, it is important to dress carefully in order to avoid excessive chilling and frostbite. If you are likely to encounter these conditions frequently, you should invest in a beautifully made pair of one-piece long underwear. They're expensive, but well worth the price. Ours are 20 percent Angora rabbit, 45 percent wool, and 35 percent acrylic. They breathe and bend without stretching, wash easily, and never, but never, part company at waist level. The zippers (one runs full length in the front, one triggers a drop-seat in the rear) have yet to give us a minute's trouble.

One final word for the ladies while we're here in the lingerie department: If at all feasible, go braless. With all the other layers you'll be donning, no one will notice (if you even care) and your comfort level will rise ten notches.

There is probably nothing more vital to outdoor winter comfort than having the proper footwear. Warm, dry, comfortable feet are essential. We *always* wear two pairs of socks. Almost everyone agrees that the outer pair should be a thick wicking type where, theoretically, perspiration is "wicked" upward to evaporate into the outside air. If you'll be wearing knickers, you should also wear knee-length socks made especially for plus fours. These will be your outer pair in this case.

As to the inner pair, opinions vary. I've tried the nylon variety, lightweight wool, and even the stretch-terry socks worn under tennis shoes. They all work. In fact, since I have a narrow foot and most boots come only in a medium width, I often wear three pairs of socks. All this cushioning makes any reasonably constructed boot feel custom made and precludes any blisters at all.

Well, there you are, clad in underwear and socks. Now what? The shirt. If this is one of the milder days, wear a cotton knit turtleneck shirt. It's absorbent, not too warm, and the higher neck will protect your skin from chaffing by the layer to follow. If, on the other hand, it's cold outside, choose a wool shirt. Wool's qualities are well known and appreciated by anyone who pays heed to the wind-chill factor. A 100-percent wool shirt will do, as will a wool and synthetic-fiber blend, either woven or knitted.

Now for the pants. It is traditional to wear knickers, and for good reasons. There hasn't been a pair of pants designed which allows for greater movement and comfort. On the other hand, it's

Knickers are the traditional wear of cross-country skiers. No other legwear allows as much comfort and flexibility. The knee-length socks are worn in addition to an inner pair for extra warmth and protection against blisters.

unlikely that you already own knickers, and while you may choose to purchase a pair at some future date, don't postpone your skiing on this account.

A warmish day? Wear jeans or any loose-fitting casual trousers. If you'll wear long underwear under them, be sure the pants are large enough to accommodate the extra bulk without restricting movement. Roomy wool slacks will do; extra fullness at the bottom can be tucked into your socks, held close with a rubber band or covered with gaiters (which we'll get to later). Wool, of course, will remain warm when wet, while cotton/synthetic will not.

The final layer you'll need for the bulk of the day is a sweater or a vest. Leave all acrylic sweaters at home. The colors are nice, the loft if often superb, and they're easy to launder, but leave them back beside the fireplace. Here 100-percent wool is definitely recommended. A pullover is generally worn, probably in a loose knit, but there's no reason a cardigan wouldn't do as well. The very best sweaters are those knit of yarn processed to retain much of the natural lanolin. Beads of moisture can be brushed from the surface of these sweaters and at the same time they allow evaporation of your own body moisture.

Goose-down vests are worn more and more instead of sweaters.

There is no possible binding under the arm here, they're light-weight, and, when fitted properly, cover the kidney area. When you are on the move over the snow you'll never miss the extra cover on your arms.

There is another item of importance and that is a very light-weight shell jacket. Wear one of nylon, of cotton poplin, or of a cotton and synthetic combination in a tight weave. You probably will never wear the jacket while moving, but going and coming and during rest stops they're invaluable for keeping the warm air next to you and the chilling wind outside. The jacket should be light enough to tie around your waist when not needed or crammed into a pack. (We'll cover packs in another chapter.)

Some snowshoers/skiers recommend warm-up pants, which do keep you warm when motionless but are generally unnecessary. I own a pair, but I rarely use them for active sports, being com-fortable in long underwear and pants. If you already own a pair and carrying them won't be a problem, bring 'em. Otherwise they're an item you can well do without.

Now, as to boots. They're very different in each of our two snow sports. Let us consider cross-country skiing first; it's simpler. Skis, bindings, and boots should all be purchased together to en-sure that all the components fit together. Cross-country ski boots are likely to be very comfortable, more comfortable than even sneakers. The whole idea here is softness and flexibility, so if your foot zigs or zags where the normal foot doesn't, the boot is supple enough to accommodate itself to your shape. Especially since you are wearing those two pairs of socks we mentioned earlier. The only thing the ski boot cannot do is reduce the height of the counter. So if your heel is shallow (shoes often rub under the ankle bone) just glue in a felt heel pad and *voilà*, comfort.

One very handy item to own is a pair of gaiters. Gaiters look very much like the spats worn by dapper gentlemen in times past, but instead of suede they are fashioned of water-repellent fabric like duck. They cover that vulnerable area at the boot top. It is just here that snow will accumulate and eventually melt, running disgustingly through the sock to wet and chill the entire foot. Gaiters also cover the boot laces, leaving them dry and easy to loosen at the end of the day. This is especially welcome when hands are chilled, the sun sinking, and the wind rising. Gaiters come in two lengths: long, which comes almost to the knee, and short, which covers the boot top by several inches.

Boots for snowshoeing are quite another matter. Here you must think not only of your feet but of the snowshoes as well. Whether you wear the traditional thong snowshoe or the new aluminum and vinyl Sherpas, the heel of your boot collides with the body of the snowshoe with each step. Obviously the webbing or sheeting will be subject to far too much abuse if the boot heel is raised and has sharp edges. Snowmobile boots are a possible choice if you already own a pair, but they won't suit the purpose for long; they're simply too hot and clumsy for anything but short-distance tours. Cross-country ski boots, while they have a fine heel, don't offer enough support for the foot, and soft hiking boots, while sturdy and comfortable enough, have that abrasive heel. Where does that leave us?

For the purist on cold, powdery snow, several pairs of wool socks are sufficient. Norwegian slipper-socks will also do if you can manage the bindings, but there are two better choices. The first is a pair of shoe pacs with rubber bottoms and leather tops. They will keep your feet dry even when the snow melts, while the leather uppers serve to provide some ventilation. The heels are smoothly rounded, which prolongs the life of the snowshoes. Another good choice is a pair of felt boots. These can be worn alone (but with socks, of course), or, in sloshy conditions, under a pair of Arctics, also known as galoshes.

Especially recommended by some are high-rising Indian moccasins. If you are lucky enough to be able to find these, by all means try them. Chrome-tanned are the best for very cold, dry snow, while oil-treated are more waterproof.

Hats are an important item of outdoor winter apparel. They're inexpensive, colorful, and vital—not necessarily in that order. Maybe no other single piece of clothing matters as much as the hat. Hat on, ears covered, and you're warm. More heat is dissipated from the head than any other single area of the body. The frost you often see on a skier's hat or hair is proof of the great amount of moisture and heat escaping from the scalp. If the snowshoer/skier feels he's getting too warm, he should remove his hat immediately. Done quickly enough, it prevents perspiration from accumulating and fends off future chill. Obviously, the opposite is

A good wool cap is essential, as nothing does more to retain body heat. Mittens or gloves are just as important. Both head and hands should be covered and uncovered as frequently as changing conditions demand.

true. If the hatless outdoorsman feels the chill, covering the head will make a greater, faster difference than donning any other item of clothing.

The traditional headgear is the tuque (pronounced to͞ok) and is of Canadian origin. This is the familiar loosely knitted cap with the tassel. Tassels add nothing that a pom-pom won't, and neither is vital (except maybe as a handle); both look perky. Wool is the preferred material again, and a hat that will pull down over your ears is important. A nice, bright red, orange, or acid-green makes you easy to spot from a distance. That fact might be important one day.

Some people just seem to suffer from cold ears more than others, and for this reason an earband is nice to have. It can be worn in addition to or instead of the hat, depending on weather conditions. Frostbitten ears, like toes, are no joke, and you can't wiggle your ears, as you can toes, to warm them.

Hands, like heads, can and should be covered and uncovered as frequently as conditions demand. Like the rest of the body, hands will warm up with physical exertion, but being at the far end of the heat line, they will cool off quicker and warm up more slowly than other parts. Mittens are warmer than gloves. A pair with a knitted body and leather palm, or all leather with a foam and acrylic lining is our favorite. The warmest of all is a two-part combination: gloves or mittens of wool knit next to the hand and a waterproof and windproof material as the outer shell. In most instances, however, this will be more warmth than you'll need. The newest type of glove is made with leather palm and a ventilated cotton body. The less expert a skier or snowshoer you are, the greater the desirability of a snug wrist on either gloves or mittens.

We have said all through this section on clothing that it just isn't necessary to approach snowshoeing and cross-country skiing fully armed with specific clothing. A wide variety of articles, most of which you probably already own, will do the job. The idea is enjoyment on the snow, and the costume is purely functional. The same holds true with sunglasses. Some protection is necessary for your comfort and safety, but just exactly what to wear depends entirely on you.

Let us first consider what you may currently own. About the only thing that absolutely will not do would be tiny lenses in a bluish or pinkish shade. Lens size is important, as the greatest visual hazard on the snow is glare. No matter what the color or density of the lens, if it's small, glare penetrates from lens edges. Also, the eye is drawn to the contrast line at the sides, and it is therefore difficult to concentrate on the terrain ahead.

Color is also important and that blue, pink, red range is least desirable. Grey, grey-green or dark green is best, as these shades don't upset the natural color balance. Amber or yellow is rec-- ommended for overcast days, as they enable the wearer to see humps and dips in the snow, and better avoid spills.

You may already own photochromic glasses, those which darken in bright sun and lighten in dull light. These will be satisfactory except on the brightest days. On these very brilliant days a lens with 85 to 90 percent absorption is best, and the photochromic lenses only darken to 60 percent at best. (By the way, they never darken in the presence of ultraviolet rays that are blocked by glass, so if you are considering investing in this type of spectacle, be aware that they will not darken while you're driving a car, in a boat's cockpit, or in the cockpit of an airplane.)

You may well own prescription sunglasses. Such glasses, pre- scribed by a professional, are likely to be best. They are probably a large lens, and the glass can be treated so that it is break-resistant and filters out ultraviolet rays. Also, being glass, the tints are stable, which they are not on most plastic lenses. If you are wearing bifocals, however, you will find that the ground in front of you is blurred at about 15 feet, just where you will be looking. In this case it might be advisable to have a pair made up for you using only your distance prescription. You probably won't be reading any fine print while touring, anyway.

Polarized sunglasses will do you no harm, but they are made to block glare from flat surfaces such as a plate glass window, sheet metal, or the surface of the water. On the snow, glare is reflected from each individual crystal and therefore enters the eye from a myriad of angles, only one of which will be blocked by these lenses.

If you wear contact lenses to correct vision—wonderful. Keep them in place, but since you are probably more sensitive than most to light, wear a non-prescription pair of sunglasses along with the contacts. The sunglasses should be in a deep shade of grey.

We have all seen those sunglasses which are mirrored on the outside. These are ordinary lenses which, instead of being im- pregnated with dyes, are coated. Coating allows complete freedom in determining just where and how deep the shading will be. This is especially important for those on the snow since even more light

Mirror-coated sunglasses often feature "gradient density," with the top and bottom thirds offering greater glare protection than the center third. This is especially good for skiers and snowshoers, who must contend with both the sun and its reflection off the snow.

is reflected into the eye from the snow below eye level than from the sun above. This is why a brimmed hat won't do the entire job of shading the eyes. The coated lenses are available with "gradient density," which only means that the top and bottom thirds of the lens are more heavily coated than the center portion. A very comfortable arrangement for double glare situations.

In recent years, with downhill skiing popularity reaching all-time heights and now cross-country skiing growing at a very rapid pace, special ski goggles have come on the market. If you feel that the sunglasses you now have will not be satisfactory, look into the possibility of buying these plastic goggles.

Happily, plastic inherently decreases the amount of ultraviolet rays reaching your eyes. This protects you from snow-blindness, except at high altitudes and for extended periods of exposure. Under these conditions you *must* be extremely fussy about your eye protection, remembering that the harmful rays are just as powerful on dull days as bright.

Goggles usually come in yellows and amber shades and, as mentioned earlier, these show shadows in greater detail. Some

Plastic ski goggles offer excellent protection and plenty of shade to the top and sides.

have interchangeable lenses so when the light is too bright for the paler shades you may change to a high-density filter. Some are designed to fit over your own glasses.

Any goggle should fit snugly, both to prevent glare from sneaking in the edges and for protection from sudden snow or sleet storms or passing branches. It should also provide a wide range of vision. Choose a flat-surfaced goggle instead of the bubble; there's far less distortion.

You will find that whatever eye protection you choose there will be problems with fogging up. Manufacturers, both domestic and foreign, know that if they could just come up with a solution to this problem they'd have the market to themselves and believe me, they've tried. They've tried everything from double layers to windshield wipers, and so far have been wholly unsuccessful.

What to do? There are several choices: One, suffer. Two, carry a paper napkin or linen handkerchief and wipe, or three, bring two pairs of glasses or goggles and switch back and forth. Sometimes ventilating the sides by some means is useful. If you discover a better solution, patent it—you'll be rich.

For more complete information on outdoor eye needs and how to supply them, see James Gregg's book, *The Sportsman's Eye*, published by Winchester Press.

5

Skis or Snowshoes?

THE IMPORTANT ROLE that snowshoes once played in human af-
fairs has become more and more obscured by the smog of the
internal combustion engine which, conversely, has become more
and more indispensable. As noted previously, peoples of the Arctic
regions were totally dependent on the webbed devices. And most
of the American and European expeditions to reach both the North
and South Poles by Peary, Amundsen, Franklin, and their con-
temporaries placed varying dependence on snowshoe travel.

Snowshoes have participated in many rescue missions. In the
early days of coast-to-coast train travel across the United States,
it wasn't uncommon for trains to be stalled for days by sudden
storms in the High Sierras or Rocky Mountains, stranding whole
trainloads of passengers who weren't used to such sub-zero hard-
ships. One westbound Southern Pacific trainload was saved from
certain starvation and exposure by a relief party arriving on snowshoes. However, this one was unusual, having been organized by
William Randolph Hearst's *Examiner*. It made a sensational, typi-
cally Hearstian news story because the snowshoers came bearing
packs of caviar canapés, foie gras, and roast chicken from caterers
in Carson City on their backs.

But that may have been the last time snowshoeing made any
kind of headlines, because it really isn't a glamorous sport at all
anymore. However, it remains the best, most dependable, and,
under certain conditions, the fastest way to travel across trackless

Snowshoes give a firmer base for shooting game with camera, although skis permit a photographer to cover ground faster.

Generally we prefer snowshoes after a fresh snowfall—and for shorter trips before snow has had a chance to compact.

country which lies muffled under a deep soft snow. As a sport, it is a wonderful conditioner, an excellent means to enjoy nature, and a far greater tranquillizer than any drugs or medicines a doctor might prescribe. Even when hanging up, retired from use on a cabin wall, snowshoes have a magic and beauty which stored skis cannot match.

But is snowshoeing *better* than skiing now?

The answer, of course, is yes—and no. Aside from personal preference, temperature and snow conditions are what make the difference. Throughout every winter season, Peggy and I depend on both snowshoes and skis and often for the same purposes.

In the very beginning snowshoeing is easier to master because you only walk on webs naturally, but with a slightly wider stance. This takes a little getting used to, as it requires new muscle development in the thighs, but offers no threat to your balance whatsoever. If you can stand up on two feet, you can stand up on snowshoes. Therein is the great advantage. As a firm base for photography, I usually prefer the snowshoes for shooting any wildlife that may be somewhat nervous.

Backpackers can carry heavier loads in greater safety on snowshoes. And I would not want to have been on skis when I carried a field-dressed, quartered moose from where it was shot far from a hunting camp to the nearest road accessible by car. But we managed with snowshoes. Heavy weights *can* be carried on skis by a skilled skier, but snowshoes do the job better. Recently during Idaho's open season, a hunter marooned in remote high country by a heavy snowfall died of a heart attack. Separate parties of veteran skiers, snowshoers, and men on horseback were dispatched to bring out the body. Two snowshoers working together reached the spot first, carried the hunter out from a place the horsemen and skiers couldn't even reach.

Snowshoeing is best over a fresh, new or deep snow that is unbroken—the same condition in which a skier might sink hopelessly. Skiing is always better when there is a track to follow. For example, the second skier in a line has it easier than the first who is breaking trail. The third skier has it even easier and so on, because the snow becomes more compacted and the surface more suitable for gliding. More than once when skiing following a recent snow, I have been thankful for a snowshoer's track to follow.

Snowshoeing is obviously a lot slower. It is unesoteric and

Snowshoeing is really nothing more than walking with long wide strides.

dependable rather than a swift means to cross country. Per mile, usually, it also requires more effort. Unless you consciously maintain a deliberately slow and steady pace, you tire too quickly.

Now let's explore the completely uncomplicated technique of snowshoeing. One important rule must be observed: Consider that you absolutely cannot walk when one shoe is holding the other down. Therefore pick up one foot/shoe and move it ahead far enough over the other never to come down on the other. This may mean slightly longer strides (the length depends on the size of the snowshoe) with feet wider apart than normal. Once you get into the habit of it, you soon travel without ever thinking about that problem of tripping up. Otherwise snowshoeing on the level is just walking.

The first trial steps should be taken on a tramped out or hardened surface. Next go to softer, deeper snow and try it, being careful to put the heels down ahead of the toes; this keeps the front tips from collecting snow. If too much snow is collected or the boot toe rubs against anything, it may be necessary to check and tighten the bindings.

Some snowshoers prefer two poles (see the guide for selection in Chapter 3), some only one, others none at all. They're not absolutely essential, but one can come in handy. Anyway if using two,

For climbing in deep snow and high country as here, snowshoes get the nod over cross-country skis. They are better also when packing into the mountains. Photo by Bill Prater.

move the right pole ahead with the left foot and vice versa, but do not thrust hard to push ahead as in skiing. Poles come in handiest when, eventually, the snowshoer falls down. Getting up again can be a little difficult in fluffy deep snow, which may seem bottomless.

If a snowshoer is not alone, the best way to get up is by a

helpful hand from somebody else. Maybe there is a handy tree or bush for a pull-up. If solid base can be touched with the pole, use it as a vertical prop to stand erect. If not, lay the ski pole horizontal on the surface and grasp it at mid-point for the push upward.

It is possible to negotiate fairly steep slopes on snowshoes just by angling rather than walking straight up the face. Or make switch-backs (a diagonal Z-shaped trail up the hill), sidestepping up the very steepest places (as when skiing). This also is called traversing. Almost any hillside can be conveniently tackled just by selecting and planning the route well ahead, watching for the best gradient.

Turning is best done exactly as skiers do it, except that (snow-shoes being shorter) it is easier. Do it by the step-turn method, planting one ski at a time part way in the direction to be turned until the full turn is completed. Pay attention not to put the tail of one shoe down on top of the other.

Because most snowshoe travel takes place on softer snow than does skiing, the snowshoes sink down to some extent with each step. It therefore is a good idea to walk deliberately, pausing ever so briefly after putting down each foot, rather than trying to tread lightly in hopes of not sinking in. The slight pause causes snow underfoot to compact or change structure, and gives the snowshoer a firmer launch pad for the next step.

Some Indian snowshoers (who are used to traveling long dis-tances to run traplines) always walk with a rolling motion of the whole body which shifts weight from side to side. These men sel-dom hurry, but plod at a speed they can maintain all day long without undue fatigue. That is a good example to imitate.

Steep downhill slopes should be approached and tackled with caution. Avoid going straight down (go diagonally instead) unless the bindings fit perfectly and are tight on the boots. Otherwise the toe might dig in under the crossbar and result in a headlong pitch into the snow. On some moderate slopes with fairly hard snow, it is possible to sit down on the shoes and slide down the hill as if on a sled or skis. But it's not a good idea if you're carrying a loaded rucksack on your back.

Together, cross-country skiing and snowshoeing require—and indeed produce—a higher level of physical fitness than any other sports, including running, jogging, cycling, swimming, Alpine ski-ing, tennis, golf, and weight lifting. Skiing and snowshoeing have the advantage because they thoroughly exercise all of the body's

Traction-bottom snowshoes give travelers a secure grip on terrain that has been packed hard by stiff mountain winds. Photo by Bill Prater.

major muscle groups: those in the arms, back, abdomen, and chest, as well as those in the legs.

Keep in mind that physical fitness here does not mean bulging muscles and massive strength. Rather it refers to how well the body performs, how well, for example, the heart and lungs cooperate to make the muscles function. When the level of physical fitness is raised high enough, it provides some protection against heart attacks. Snowshoeing and cross-country skiing also are aerobic activities and, therefore, excellent activities for controlling weight. Stored body fat is used up. It is a rare thing to see an active cross-country skier who is also chubby. Girl-watching may nowhere be more rewarding than along a snowshoe or ski-touring trail.

The wise skier and snowshoer begins to get in shape well before the snow season begins. That is especially true for ski racers or mountaineers. But even recreational skiers can have a lot more fun by skiing farther and faster without noticeable fatigue.

Training for the snow season does not have to be an ordeal, or even unpleasant. It simply means being *more* active than normal. It could mean walking to work every day (or at least part of the way) instead of riding. It could mean always walking up steps at the office instead of taking the elevator. It can mean swimming, jogging, biking, playing handball or tennis if you happen to be confined to town and the facilities of the athletic club. The emphasis should always be to exercise often, regularly, and in moderation, rather than sporadically and very strenuously.

But let's admit here that to suddenly start snowshoeing or cross-country skiing—or to start training seriously for either—could conceivably be dangerous. People over 40 or so who have been sedentary or overweight for a long time, heavy drinkers or smokers, anyone with a latent or potential heart condition, should begin with greatest caution. Fortunately cardiologists can detect heart problems by EKG tests and recommend physical activity accordingly. But given a sound heart, out-of-condition people can start shaping up just by walking regularly. Start on a fixed program, say of six to eight weeks. Every day for the first week walk one mile in 20 minutes, swinging your arms and flexing arm muscles. Increase that energy output gradually each week until during the final week you are walking two miles in 30 minutes or less. That pace is something virtually everyone can attain. If it seems too easy, jog part of the way. Or eventually do your walking in hilly or rough terrain rather than on level ground. Or borrow junior's bike to test leg muscles even more. One skier we know used the nearby high school football stadium to tone up his leg muscles, by both jogging around the cinder track and then climbing up and down the rows of spectator seats. By increasing the number of climbs each day, his legs were soon in superlative shape, and it was all accomplished without leaving his own suburban neighborhood.

Remember, though, that arms may furnish as much as a quarter of the propulsion in ski touring, and they should be exercised too. Peggy and I have found that in the beginning of each snow season our arms fatigue far faster than our legs because we have been hiking and day packing throughout the summer. But our arms haven't been used that much.

A good way to condition chest and arms is to walk directly up steep hills, using the ski poles to help push ahead exactly as if skiing. Again, start modestly, and gradually increase both the time and energy spent. Of course, if you feel foolish ski-poling in shorts amid the autumn leaves (though you really shouldn't in these uninhibited times) retreat to your basement and attach a pair of elastic stretch or exercising bands to the wall at just above shoulder height. Next step back several feet and with your arms alternately stretch out the bands in exactly the same rhythm you use when skiing. Increase the exercise each day. It is a splendid way to tune up arms, trunk, and shoulders, even if you don't care to ski or snowshoe.

Very serious skiers—racers mostly—can train the year around on roller skis. These have small ratcheted (to prevent rolling backward) wheels mounted on normal skis and can be used on paved or very smooth surfaces.

Snowshoers can get their legs in shape the same way as skiers, but with one extra refinement, by wearing metal training or boxer's weights on their shoes. They can don these whenever doing garden chores, walking the dog, out hunting in the late fall, even when walking to work. The extra weight on the boot makes the transition to wearing snowshoes almost unnoticeable when winter comes.

How much skiing or snowshoeing is enough for you? How far can you safely go?

According to Dr. C. Joseph Cross, Columbus, Ohio, internist and heart specialist, you are proceeding at an ideal and healthy pace if you feel pleasantly tired after a session on webs or skis. You can figure on some stiffness or soreness after a good workout, but this should disappear with a hot bath or shower. To go beyond that—to have *really* stiff and sore nagging muscles—is stretching it too far. Slow down until you are more fit. As you ski or snowshoe more and more, you'll also enjoy it more.

6

Ski-Touring Techniques

THE FIRST PLACE PEGGY AND I ever clamped on our cross-country skis was at Snow Lodge, within sight of Old Faithful in Yellowstone National Park. It was mid-February, snow was piled eight feet deep on the level, and we had paused there during a cross-park trip via one of the snow cruisers operated by the Yellowstone Park Company. In recent years, thanks to these cruises (and keeping the Lodge open all year long), it is possible for tourists to see one of the world's most remarkable natural wonders in winter. That's when the scenery is most spectacular and big-game animals are easier to observe at close range than at any other time.

Still a tourist is handicapped, as we found, unless he has a means of getting out and away from the Lodge and its cleared paths, all of which lead only toward Old Faithful. Fortunately we met Van Tribble, a ski instructor there who was then renting skis and snowshoes to visitors.

"Try a pair of our touring skis," he suggested, "and you can mingle right among the elk and buffalo."

Along with a group of eight or nine other complete novices, Peggy and I listened and watched through an hour's explanation and demonstration of skis. To this date that's all the formal instruction we ever had—and perhaps it wasn't nearly enough. When out on our own, we felt uncertain at first and fell down often. That would have been embarrassing except that the other beginners were also tumbling in the soft snow. But we soon learned to stand up on skis and move out.

Suddenly, it seemed, we had the knack. We were striking out smoothly, maintaining balance, feeling secure. In fact we soon were doing well enough that I risked carrying a motor-driven Nikon camera with telephoto lens around my neck. I'd discovered something really fine and exhilarating, something that looked hard but wasn't.

That same afternoon we skied around the nearby geyser basin to the Firehole River and paralleled it for a distance northward and downstream. The Firehole is one of the most fantastic waterways on earth, a place where an angler could conceivably catch and cook (it's not legal, though) a trout, all while standing in the same spot. In winter, however, it is an even more extraordinary spectacle.

Hissing steam and scalding water rushing from hot springs along both banks not only prevents the river from freezing, but condenses on the nearest trees and transforms them into grotesque white pyramids. And scattered about in this unreal, ghostly scene was a herd of elk bedded in the snow.

A few of the elk, including one handsome old bull, drifted away at our approach, but not very far before bedding again. Most paid no attention as we focused from closer and closer range. A few didn't even bother to arise from their beds as we skied right among them. A person might spend a good part of his life hunting wildlife with a camera around the world and never have a more intimate glimpse of America's second largest deer—or any other large wild animal. Still more was to follow.

Further along the Firehole we abruptly came upon a pair of bison. I say abruptly because both were lying down and so completely covered up with snow as to be camouflaged white mounds. The two stood up only when we were practically on top of them, stared at us dully for a few moments and then the huge shaggy beasts waded to the far side of the Firehole where we couldn't follow.

That evening back at Snow Lodge I felt soreness deep in my legs from muscles which hadn't been used recently. Shoulders also complained from plying the poles. But it was bittersweet pain there beside an open fire because I'd shot several rolls of otherwise elusive photo subjects in exquisite backgrounds. And as stated before, I'd discovered cross-country skiing.

Almost anyone could learn to ski just as easily—or more easily. At that time I was just past 50 and because of an outdoor life was in good physical condition but had never been on any kind of skis before. It is so easy to learn that countless acquaintances of ours have taught themselves just by trial and error.

However, the best bet for a beginner is to enlist correct instruction from an expert teacher when that is possible. Nowadays lessons for neophytes are available free (or at least very inexpensively) in many places, such as the popular downhill-ski resorts, YMCAs, sporting-goods stores, ski-touring and athletic clubs, adult physical education centers, and high school and college physical education departments. Check out all the possibilities where you live; some may exist just next door.

But let's suppose that no formal instruction happens to be handy. You can still proceed on your own, especially if you obtain a good instruction manual. One such ("Ski Touring Guide") is available for $1.50 from the American Ski Touring Council, West Hill Road, Troy, Vermont 05868.

With guide in hand, go to any park, golf course, playing field, or otherwise fairly level bit of open real estate. Wax your skis and put them on. First follow the instructions in your book for traveling in a straight line, then gradually try out and practice turns, slightly uphill and down. Given moderate coordination and some patience, these moves are not difficult. Suddenly all will seem to be second nature.

The basic motion to try to achieve is the smooth glide forward. With skis parallel, try shoving one foot out strongly ahead of the other and coast on it. But before the coast dies out, bring the other foot from behind and shove it out front in the same manner. That way, gradually accelerating, you will be surprised at the rapid, effortless way you can cover ground. You will do better if you lift the rear foot from the snow slightly so that the ski skims forward, barely brushing the snow.

It is sound advice (unless you are very young, agile, and athletic) to start out slowly and in small doses. Ski-touring, like swimming, is a "total exercise," and will bring into play some muscles not otherwise tested. There is no point in aggravating these when gradual exercise (or prior conditioning) will develop them naturally. So stop and rest often. People who do not walk very frequently

First efforts to achieve the smooth glide forward that is ski touring should be made on level ground. It is so easy that formal instruction, though helpful, is not really necessary.

or get outdoors very often may find that a tour of three or four city blocks all at once is a long one to start.

After feeling confident and at ease on the level, a cross-country skier must learn to travel uphill and down as well. Learning to do well on downhills is mostly a matter of staying relaxed and limber as confidence builds. The proper position or stance is with knees bent and acting as shock absorbers. One experienced instructor, Almy Coggeshall, advises the following drill for downhilling:

"Set your ski pole in front of the toe, with the heels flat on the

Downhill touring is exhilarating, but a neophyte should start on gentle slopes such as this one.

skis, relax at the ankles, and let the knees sag forward until the knee touches the ski pole. Bounce up and down a little to loosen up. Next select a very short hill with the slope so gentle that skis barely slide when a trail is smoothed out. Starting well back from the top of the hill, get into stride as you go over the edge and start down. Speed will pick up, but keep your knees bent as you ride out the slope. Keep doing this over and over, eventually not breaking stride at all to build poise and balance as well as a growing confidence."

When you can manage the gentle hill easily on two skis, try shifting your weight from side to side in a rocking motion as you go down. This mastered, try lifting one ski and then the other, going on one at a time, transferring back and forth in slow easy rhythm. Gradually progress to steeper and steeper slopes, repeating the confidence drills.

On level or gently rolling ground a skier changes direction by stopping, picking one ski off the snow and setting it down at the desired angle to the track. The second ski is picked up and set down parallel to the first. Sharper turns must be accomplished in two stages although really good agile skiers can manage a 180-degree turn in a single stage. To change direction going downhill, you do essentially the same except that you're sliding. Changes of direction cannot be quite as abrupt; adding body english helps. All that lifting of one ski after the other on downhill drills will pay off here when it comes time to turn.

Proper waxing of skis, which we'll consider in detail shortly, makes skiing uphill little different than proceeding on the level. In other words, continue up any grade until almost on the point of back slipping. Switchback (zigzag) when you can. When the slope ahead is still too steep, or you have not waxed correctly, there are two old techniques to use; the herringbone and the side step.

The latter is the easiest for many skiers. This way you scale a slope sideways, moving the uphill ski first and bringing the lower ski up beside it. The resultant pattern in the snow resembles a wide staircase. To herringbone, a skier faces uphill and alternately places skis at 45-degree angles to the slope, a procedure which can be tough going after a while.

To slow down or stop when going downhill, a technique called snowplowing is used. The skier actually tilts both skis against the grain of the slope, pushing outward with his feet, but pointing the ski tips together to form a V. This acts as a very efficient brake which can be practiced first on very gentle slopes.

Up to this point we've avoided—deliberately—the mention of ski poles. There are fair reasons for it. At least one veteran cross-country ski instructor recommends not using poles at all in the beginning as a way to gain confidence faster. Some others insist that a skier is better off doing (with the ski poles) just what seems

With properly waxed skis it is possible to climb directly up modest slopes without slipping backward.

to come naturally. An entirely opposite opinion is held by most other instructors.

When a skier adds pole movements to his forward stride, he provides extra push—extra momentum—to his cross-country glide. The sequence starts as the right leg and left arm thrust forward at the same time, just as the left pole has been planted in the snow with a firm, but not necessarily tight, grip on the handle. Then, as the left ski goes forward, the left pole swings behind, a process which is much easier to demonstrate than to explain.

One point of disagreement among experts is exactly how hard

to thrust forward with the pole, how much to rely on arms versus legs for momentum. The answer probably lies within each individual, or rather on how powerful are his arms. If the upper body is in good shape, well developed, why not use it? Remember that ski poles are equally valuable in maintaining balance, as a brief holding brake when going uphill, and as a means of support for getting up after a fall.

At this point it is impossible to delay any longer the sticky subject of waxing skis. A number of efficient waxes are sold in America, but one brand, Swix, has become so popular and widely accepted that the name is often used (like jello for any gelatin) to designate ski wax in general. Following, therefore, is general waxing advice offered by Swix.

Because correct selection and application of wax are necessary for a good climbing "grip," for a fast glide and to prevent snow-clogged skis, a wax kit must be carried on all but very short runs. The first step is selection of the right wax after looking at the snow of which, for our purposes, there are three kinds. Begin with *new snow*, which forms a loose covering on the surface. New snow is gradually transformed into *fine-grained snow*, which is tighter and consists of a less rounded grain. Finally there is *coarse-grained snow* consisting of rounded, often separated, ice crystals with a large grain size. This last (for waxing purposes) is in the same category as crusted snow.

All running waxes must be applied on clean, dry skis which have been cleaned of any previous, different wax. Old wax is taken off by scraping or by a propane torch. Tube waxes—klister—among the stickiest substances man has ever devised, must be applied at room temperatures. Tinned or stick waxes can be applied at lower temperatures outdoors.

Wax must be spread evenly by rubbing with the hands (or leather gloved hands) or by using a large cork. To be spared reapplication during long trips when snow conditions are unlikely to change, put on a double layer. The following chart from Swix is a good, reliable one to use.

At least for beginners, judging—estimating—the day's skiing surface can be perplexing, and even more so when temperatures change rapidly. Begin by reading the air temperature and then judging the snow type—new snow, fine-grained snow, coarse-grained snow,

SWIX waxing table for cross-country skiing

New snow	Fine-grained "old" snow	Coarse-grained snow, crust and ice
-2°C and lower (Green Tin)	−10°C and lower (Green Tin)	Dry to moist snow (Blue Tube)
-2°C to 0°C (Blue Tin)	−10°C and 0°C (Blue Tin)	Wet snow (Violet Tube)
Beginning mild weather, abt. 0°C (Violet Tin)	Beginning mild weather, abt. 0°C (Violet Tin)	
Moist (cloggy) snow, smooth trade (Yellow Tin)	Moist snow (Red Tin)	
Wet snow (Red Tube)	Wet snow (Violet Tube)	

Printed in U.S.A. by Bodine, Inc.

or crust and ice. Below freezing-point you simply choose the wax that corresponds to the actual temperature and snow type. At an air temperature of o degrees Centigrade or warmer you have to remember that the temperatures of air and snow are not the same and that the choice of wax in this case will depend on the moisture content of the snow surface. The easiest way of judging this is to take a handful of snow in one's gloved hand: Dry snow will fall away in flakes, moist snow will pack and hold together, and wet snow will show a distinctly wet outer surface. Be particularly careful when judging the conditions at a temperature of about o degrees C. Having decided on the type of snow, you will easily find the actual wax from the Swix waxing table.

The waxing is most easily done at room temperature, and the running surface has to be dry to enable the surface-wax to adhere to the ski. The harder tin waxes should be applied with short and rather soft movements and should be spread out as evenly as possible over the whole running surface. Then spread out the wax to

With added skill and confidence, a skier can proceed over difficult or broken country with remarkable ease.

a full covering in an even and smooth layer by means of a waxing block or the handle of a ski-scraper.

That sums up basic cross-country skiing: proper waxing of the equipment and a careful beginning to build confidence. In no time at all most skiers are gliding across country faster than they ever believed possible. At the same time they're also becoming addicted to a grand new winter sport. Anybody who can walk is susceptible.

7

Cross-Country Trails and Travel

DURING A RECENT WINTER in the Northeast, a party of six cross-country skiers began what was to be an all-day tour in a semi-wilderness area. All were young, in good health, and with at least moderate skiing ability. By nightfall they had not returned to their starting base, and the next day also passed without word of them. A search was begun.

Before the skiers were found exhausted and with frostbitten feet, the state police, National Guard, Civil Air Patrol, and even units of the Naval Air Reserve were called upon to search. Altogether the rescue cost taxpayers almost a quarter million dollars—just because no one had considered taking along a contour map of the area (which wasn't really vast) and a compass.

Very few skiing or cross-country ventures, even across the more extensive unbroken wilderness areas of the West, ever end in such a crisis. And there is no need for them to end that way. By far the most skiers stick to established trails on comparatively short trips. Perhaps they may never stray beyond sight or sound of other humans—so that there is no chance at all of getting lost. Still for some skiers the whole thrill is in getting away—and the farther the better—from beaten tracks and other people. That's easy to understand. Fortunately there are countless opportunities for both in North America.

In Chapters 13 and 14 we have listed, state-by-state and Canadian province-by-province, the numerous resorts where one can find existing trails to ski. But these represent only a fraction of the total opportunities. Add to this list the summer hiking trails through northern national parks and forests, some of which are also maintained as ski and snowshoe trails. But any of the hiking and riding trails can also be traveled simply by following the familiar blazes on trees and the trail markers which hopefully are above snow level. Also, skiers can make their own trails close to or on the very edge of many towns.

Consider, for instance, all of the real estate owned by corporations, by city, county, or township governments which is not presently being used. Many mining, utility, and timber companies also own vast tracts of undeveloped land. There are also miles upon

Cross-country travel on skis or snowshoes takes the author to scenes of lonely beauty, as to this pond, kept open all winter by inflowing warm springs.

miles of abandoned rights-of-way everywhere. Often a polite formal request of the landowner or the public relations officer of the town council is the only ticket necessary to use these properties. In fact there often exists an anxiety to use idle lands for recreation or some similar benefit to the community. Why not make the most of them?

In many instances it will be necessary to "build" trails. Usually that means clearing a yard-wide path through brush, a chore that a group of skiers can complete on several weekends before snow begins to fly. Preparing trails can be a worthwhile project for local skiing and snowshoe clubs, often with help from Boy Scouts and other youth organizations. But before actually laying the trail, for which permission is necessary, keep several vital factors in mind.

First consider who will use the trail. If mostly beginners, keep it simple, on fairly level ground, and without steep hills. Always try to avoid monotony, and take greatest advantage of attractive scenery. The trail should follow an irregular and winding course so that it best takes advantage of the space available. There can be two alternate routes between points: one for beginners, the other for more advanced skiers. Remember, in planning, that you will probably want to use the trail both ways. When clearing any trail, remove only those objects absolutely necessary, and disturb the natural beauty as little as possible. Use old logging roads or cowpaths whenever practical to save both labor and the scene. Try to make the outgoing trip uphill and the return trip generally downhill if that fits into the geography.

It is true that after a heavy soft snowfall, it is a lot easier and faster to follow in the track of a snowmobile than it is to break through fresh snow. But just the same, try to avoid any contact with snowmobilers and any trail areas used by them. The philosophies of snowmobilers and skiers or snowshoers are so vastly different that there is bound to be conflict when the two groups rub too close together.

For the job of opening up trails in previously unbroken or densely wooded areas, a crew will need either a chain saw or a two-man buck saw, an axe, and one or more brush clippers. These will do most of the work clipping saplings and pruning a path ahead. Sawyers or choppers follow right behind. Teamwork will eventually get the job done better, quicker, and will also get the upper arms in better shape for using the ski poles later on.

A new snowfall makes exquisite the route of these winter travelers in the Cascades of Washington. Photo by Bill Prater.

At least some maintenance throughout winter will be required, even on the most frequently used trails. There will be storm-caused deadfalls to remove. Deep, wind-blown drifts will obliterate trails and form hummocks. In many areas where there is constant heavy traffic on the trails, the skiers alone will keep them pounded into ideal shape. But track sleds (which are really small graders) drawn by snowmobiles or tractors can be used to set and level trails for the smoothest conditions, especially after a heavy snowfall or a thaw and freeze.

It is a good idea to mark the trails at all intersections and to make a simple map of the trail network. Markers should include both destination arrows and distances so that skiers of any ability can feel confident wherever they are. You can add interest by giving colorful nostalgic or historical names to places along the trails: Bootlegger Bend, Red Deer Creek, The Indian Oak, Cattle Drive Camp, Pocahontas Point, and so on. Whenever a trail crosses a wide open space or meadow, it should be marked with poles or high rock cairns spaced within sight of each other. Remember that wind-driven snow might cover up not only the trail, but also any too-low markers.

An activity which is becoming more and more popular is the winter nature hike or bird watch on skis or snowshoes. A good many trails have been laid out with these things in mind. Unique geologic features, wildlife dens, deer yards, and unusual trees can be marked to add interest to a trip over the snow. At least one ski-touring club consulted a well-known local naturalist/biologist to help members lay out the most instructive and fascinating trail possible. Incidentally, the club had obtained permission to use the same land and build the trail from a power company that was a large landholder not too popular with environmentalists. The arrangement with the skiers helped improve the corporate image.

Some excellent examples of nature hikes on skis or snowshoes are those held weekly in Grand Teton National Park. Beginning at either the visitor center at Moose or at Colter Bay (and with webs furnished for the snowshoers) the trips are led by naturalist rangers to places where such wildlife as moose are most likely to be encountered. Many people travel long distances just to join one of these free half-day treks.

At least equally exciting for many is ski-touring after dark on a moonlit night, and that isn't any wonder. Few if any other experiences of winter can be more memorable. One still, bright, and star-studded night in a silent woods where nothing moves can be the antidote for any kind of frustration or anxiety. But plan for your night hike well ahead—and maybe as follows below.

A ranger/naturalist in Grand Teton National Park briefs group before leading a snowshoe hike near Moose visitor center.

Go out in daylight and in two or three miles from your starting point find a sheltered spot where you can pause and build a small bonfire. A cave is a good spot and so is the opening in a forest. Collect a supply of dry, dead firewood, pile it, cover it well with an old canvas cloth or plastic sheet, and leave it where you can easily find it again, even after dark. Now wait for the first clear night on a full or nearly full moon.

With a small party of friends—never with a large boisterous group—wait until nightfall and then head out toward your wood cache. It should be a wonderfully exhilarating run on what might seem to be a distant, unreal planet not unlike the pictures we've seen of the lunar surface. Maybe, if you are extremely lucky, you will be serenaded by a family of coyotes yodeling in the distance. If you are normal, that exquisite call of the wild will make bristles stand straight on the back of your neck, but there is nothing to worry about. The coyotes are only being exuberant.

This cross-country skier, carrying a rucksack full of camping gear, is prepared to stay out overnight, if that becomes necessary.

When you reach the wood cache, it's alright to cheat a little and use some artificial substance to start the fire faster. Then all sit around the blaze and cook whatever was brought along for that purpose. There is only one sad thing about it: eventually the bonfire will burn down and you will have to head homeward again. But if you've planned it properly all the way, there's a sauna or at least a hot shower waiting for the grand finale.

A few extra words of caution must be inserted about ski-touring after dark. Foremost is that nights are invariably much colder than during daylight—so dress accordingly. You need a thick cap and warmest mittens. Except when ensconced close around the fire, you absolutely have to keep moving to maintain body temperature, but not so much as to overheat, as frost crystals form on the land and the mercury plunges toward rock bottom. It isn't prudent to plan long trips at night (as is the obvious temptation) or ever to go alone. Equipment should be in good shape, skis properly waxed before starting out, and repair kits carried by all hands in case of unplanned breakdowns. Ski touring by moonlight is too remark-able an experience to be spoiled by troubles that could have been easily prevented. Also, keep all members of the party together and on the trails, because getting lost is much easier after dark.

Eventually many skiers and snowshoers will want to explore new places, to wander out into remote, mountainous, or unfamiliar country. That is always high adventure, but going out beyond established trails, even for a short distance, involves certain risks. Every skier and snowshoer should be aware of them.

Getting lost is a possibility, and the further one strays from beaten paths, the easier it is to become disoriented. Too many skiers have found that getting lost even in fairly familiar country is pos-sible; sudden storms or the onset of darkness can drastically change the looks of any place. Still there is no need for a competent skier in good health to fear traveling in lonely places—if he plans for it well.

Let's establish a set of rules here for off-trail travel. First know exactly where you are going. Obtain a topographic contour map of the area and a good reliable compass. To get the exact map or maps you need, first request the free topo map index of any state from one of the two distribution centers of the U.S. Geological Survey. For state indeces east of the Mississippi (including Min-nesota), write to U.S.G.S., 1200 S. Eads St., Arlington, Virginia 22202. For the western indeces write to U.S.G.S., Federal Center, Denver, Colorado 80225. From any index it will be easy to select the large scale topo sheets for any given area you would like to ski.

There are a good many compasses on the market ranging from cheap to very expensive. But the best we've seen for winter cross-country travel is the Sportsman, made by Uncle Mike's (Michaels) of Portland, Oregon. Although it retails for less than $20, it is a precision instrument with a lifetime guarantee. Unlike most other compasses, the Sportsman permits a skier to compensate for mag-netic declination, which varies as much as 33 degrees from true north in certain parts of northern North America.

How to use a compass correctly and accurately is too lengthy a subject to be considered in detail here. But anyone planning an ambitious winter trip had better know how to do so. One de-tailed, but clear reference on the subject is *Be Expert With Map and Compass* by Bjorn Kjellstrom, published by Scribner's. A paperback edition sells for $4.95. But even without sophisticated knowledge of how to use a compass, it will be worth its weight in gold just when indicating the general direction in a situation of great doubt.

During recent winters a number of skilled cross-country skiers have successfully skied completely across Yellowstone National Park—a distance of 100-plus miles over the rawest wilderness, and in sub-zero temperatures. Before starting out (and in fact before

Wherever required (and even when not), skiers should register trips of any duration.

the first snowfall of autumn) they had cached foodstuffs at convenient points along the way. They were also careful to notify park authorities of their exact plans.

Even though the venture may not be as heroic as crossing Yellowstone, any cross-country travelers elsewhere should do the same. If near a downhill ski area, notify the local ski patrol of any plans. Or tell friends, national forest rangers, or whatever agency is likely to be concerned if something should go wrong.

It is just as important to carry along a survival kit, either in a beltpack or day backpack. 'A' survival kits should go on every trip, even a one-day or part-day outing. It should include high-calorie food snacks, an extra layer of clothing, a fire starter and matches in a waterproof container, a pocket knife, a section of nylon rope, a first-aid kit, plus emergency repair items such as thong for snowshoes. Some cross-country explorers also carry a whistle, a colored flare, and suntan lotion in their packs. If the trip is to be longer than one day, carry a shovel, shelter, and other camping gear to be covered in the next chapter.

When planning a trip, calculate distances carefully and do not underestimate the time it will take to cover them. Especially when snowshoeing, deep drifts and windfalls can slow the pace to a fraction of what is normal. It may be necessary, wisely, to detour around places where there is the slightest chance of an avalanche. If it is hilly country, it may be essential to slow down often to keep from getting overheated. And the time required for any trip should always be calculated on the basis of the slowest, least able member of the party—not on the average speed of all.

A point too often overlooked is that of the selection of companions. The longer and more ambitious a planned winter trip, the more important it is to go with compatible people who can stand the gaff. Failure to do this has ruined more trips than failure of equipment, of getting lost, or perhaps of anything else.

Still, winter across northern North America can be a time of angry moods and the severest kind of weather to test anyone. Don't venture out beyond the point at which you lose confidence. Unless you are genuinely prepared for it, avoid getting caught out at night in a winter woods. As a psychological boost as well as valuable accessory, a Storm Kit is available from the Tacoma Unit of the Mountain Rescue Council (Box 969, Tacoma, Washington 98401). The kit weighs 11 ounces and sells for $2; Storm Shelter

A happy ending for a group ski tour in the Tetons.

Kits are also available ($1 each). They weigh next to nothing and could save your life.

Cross-country skiers should know basic first-aid. Courses can be taken in many places, usually free, and sponsored by the Red Cross, local fire and emergency departments, Boy Scouts, fish and game departments, or adult education centers. Every fall, ski patrols at downhill skiing centers offer two- or three-day refresher courses in first-aid. Attend one. But remember that most emergencies are likely to come in the form of frostbite rather than bodily injuries. Fortunately frostbite can be prevented easily.

The extremities— feet and fingers—always get cold first. But don't let them get uncomfortably—or even dangerously—cold in the first place. One way to warm numb fingers is to add whatever shirt or sweater is not being worn, and then to swing both arms vigorously in full circles. Fifty or so revolutions should warm the fingers considerably.

Cold toes are not quite so easily warmed. If traveling more rapidly doesn't work, loosening your boot laces might restore some circulation. With laces open, try jumping up and down in place. If that fails, stop and build a fire, keeping it small (confined) to concentrate the heat on your feet (boots removed, of course) while you sit close. At the same time rub your feet. Once the toes are warm again, get moving as soon as possible and—as always— try for that ideal constant pace which holds body temperature.

Cross-country travel across a snowy landscape few others ever see can be one of any winter's greatest rewards, a reward to be savored, but savored with care and respect.

8

Camping and Overnighting

On a bitter day in February several winters ago, Peggy and I began a project that must have caused some neighbors to doubt our sanity. With the temperature hovering at 10 degrees Fahrenheit in mid-afternoon, we dug a rectangular pit in the snow drifts just behind the Lazy B. It was no small chore, considering that the snow was waist-deep. When our shovels rang against the rock-hard frozen ground beneath, we pitched a light nylon mountain tent in the excavation.

That night we cooked dinner and slept in the tent while the mercury plunged to below zero. I suppose there is nothing really startling about that, except that it was a first. We have spent a good bit of time camping around the world from South Africa to the Arctic and many assorted places, hot and cold, dry and humid, and in between. That also includes a good many Rocky Mountain hunting camps in late autumn when the weather wasn't exactly benevolent. But we had never before spent a night under canvas in a near zero environment. Before starting out on more ambitious camping trips via skis or snowshoes, it seemed like good sense to have a trial run right in our own backyard. If the cold proved too great, well, we were right there at home.

Thanks mostly to a double Arctic down sleeping bag on top of three-inch polyurethane foam mattresses, it wasn't bad at all—until I had to crawl out and start breakfast in the morning, an act that was delayed until later than normal. But the trial run did prove that mid-winter camping in extremely cold conditions was practical, if not pure joy. It also made the next step a lot easier—and confident.

Perhaps the best advice for anyone planning a winter campout on skis is to try it as we did first. Some will undoubtedly find camping not worth the effort, and surely not one of the better reasons for skiing. But others will consider it an extraordinary way to savor winter at its loneliest—the North American environment at its most hostile. Go camping this way for a while and you soon get some true idea about how Eskimoes and northern Indians barely eked out an existence in ages past. It also makes you better appreciate, at the end of a camping trip, the absolute comfort of an insulated and electrically heated home.

For still others, winter camping is a test and challenge—a personal survival contest. Compare it to climbing difficult peaks, scuba diving to seldom attained depths, kayaking a wild river, or sailing the ocean in a small craft. But no matter what the reason for winter camping on touring-skis or webs, it is another of those activities for which planning is absolutely essential. Sound preparation becomes the difference between a great adventure and a terrible ordeal.

Obviously, specialized and usually expensive gear will be necessary. (But any serious, experienced backpacker may already own everything he needs.) In addition to the clothing and skis/snowshoes already described, a cold-weather camper requires shelter, a bed, food, and cooking gear, plus something to carry it in. Let's consider the items one at a time.

A snow traveler can either carry along his shelter or make it where he camps. In other words, he can lug a tent in his pack, build an igloo, or dig a snow ice cave. In a few scattered places there are natural caves to use, or abandoned cow camps, mine shafts, and trappers' cabins which can be utilized. Building an igloo or digging a cave is energy- and time-consuming, but for some purists looking for challenge, it is the most comfortable as well as the only way to go. More on how to build them later.

Almost any of the good, nylon backpack tents with light aluminum framing and built-in waterproof floors might serve for winter camping if pitched in a sheltered place, cleared of snow and out of savage winds. But far better are the mountain expedition tents of nylon, designed particularly for extremely low tem-

Lucky circumstance here on an overnight snowshoe hike permits pitching tent in a sandstone cave. You should take advantage of these places whenever possible.

peratures. There are far too many of these on the market nowadays to describe separately, but the good ones have several things in common: an over-the-top fly which creates an insulating space between tent and fly; a low, wind-resistant silhouette when erected; and a high price tag—about $150–200 for a double tent. One of these, the Overniter (a backpacking version of a Mt. Everest Expedition tent), by Eddie Bauer of Seattle, has an on-the-trail weight of ten pounds. That is on the heavy side, but it comes packed in two separate stuff bags so that the load can be split between two skiers or snowshoers. The two-man Alpine expedition tent made by Eureka is an excellent choice.

When buying a winter tent, look for the double-wall feature

Mountain tent with low, sloping silhouette to resist wind is pitched with a view of the magnificent Rockies in the background.

(which may be catalogued as a tent with fly). Because of the air space between walls, the breathing of occupants does not precipitate inside the tent and cause an uncomfortable moisture problem. Look also for shock cord ties to dissipate the force of wind. When pitching a tent for just one night, it is necessary only to pack the snow tightly underneath, rather than to clear it away completely. But for longer than that, clear out a spot. Either metal or tough plastic pegs will be necessary to stake the tent securely into frozen ground. Do not depend on finding peg material where you camp.

Despite its weight a small stove is a lot more sensible and dependable than firewood for snow camp cooking. In some places it may not be permissible to use wood anyway. Besides, stoves which

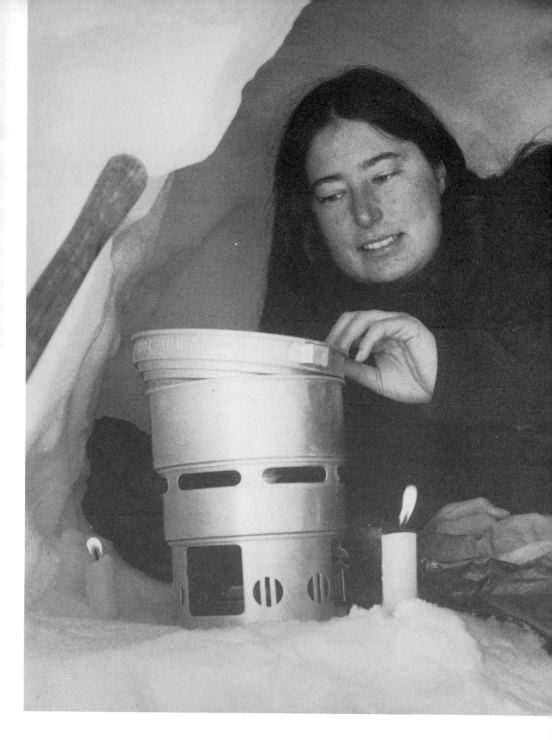

Ensconced in her ice cave, skier uses candles and lightweight aluminum cooker to prepare meal and stay comfortably warm.

use kerosene, gasoline, alcohol, butane, and propane are available, though most of the more experienced skiers prefer the gasoline stove with a pump. Kerosene smells bad in the damp confines of a tent; alcohol does not give sufficient heat; butane freezes when the temperature dips below 15 degrees Fahrenheit. The two most widely used winter stoves today are the Optimus 111B, which weighs 54 ounces, and the Phoebus 625, which is newer on the market and weighs 40 ounces. A third choice might be the Primus Grasshopper, which heats with propane.

No single development of the last several years has made backpacking more pleasant and more possible, winter or summer, than freeze-dried foods. These are available in all ski and mountain shops, most sporting goods stores, from outdoor outfitters, and even in many supermarkets. Some of the brand names of reliable products are Mountain House, Rich Moor, Chuck Wagon, Seidel's Trail Package, Stow-A-Way, and Trail Chef. These come in an endless variety of menus, from lasagna and beef stroganoff to mexicali corn and even ice cream, which can be "munched" dry along the way. When planning, figure two pounds of freeze-dried foods per person per day (or slightly more for extraordinary appetites).

There is one drawback to using freeze-dried (or any dehydrated, lightweight) foods: They're expensive. Some of the cost can be shaved by buying in quantity directly from the manufacturers, or by buying dehydrated foods at the supermarket and repacking them in plastic or aluminum foil for handier backpacking. (Some items can be packed inside the one or two aluminum cooking pots you will require.)

You can't possibly enjoy ski or snowshoe camping without getting a good night's sleep every night, something which is impossible without a warm sleeping bag. Of all gear used to go winter camping, never skimp on the purchase of a sleeping bag.

But what is the ideal bag? It should be lightweight, compressible to small size for packing, water repellent, warm, and able to "breathe" to allow body moisture to escape. All this translates into an eider or goose down-filled bag with nylon outer and inner shells, preferably in an unzippered mummy shape. This type of mummy is the warmest, most efficient for really cold situations, but it does have drawbacks.

Some people cannot sleep comfortably with feet always held

A great variety of prepared, freeze-dried, and dehydrated foods is available on the market today. Most of them are expensive, but they certainly make backpacking easier.

close together as in a mummy, and their bags should be of another shape, but nevertheless of down. Second best bet would be a zippered mummy with a plastic zipper which opens at either end. A cold-weather bag should contain four or more pounds of down constructed of (to use the trade term for it) overlapping V-tube compartments. Such bags will sell for $100 or more. Some reliable manufacturers or distributors of high-quality bags are Gerry, Arctic Designs, Sierra Designs, and Eddie Bauer. Besides the bag, a skier's bed should include a two- or three-inch styrofoam pad mattress, at least from hips to shoulder length.

The summer mountain rucksacks with metal frames can be used in winter and especially by snowshoers. However, the center of gravity at the shoulder is so high that it could make these risky for skiing in steep or difficult terrain. Probably the best carrier for most skiers is the long and narrow nylon rucksack that fits snugly and sets lower on the back than a summer packsack. Many of the most experienced skiers are selecting teardrop-shaped bags, without exterior framing for the best balance. In bitter weather zippers are far handier to work than straps or buckles, but they should be of nylon rather than metal and covered over with protective flaps. Any winter bag should be of waterproof nylon, though it may be necessary to treat the seams with some kind of waterproofing sealer.

My old friend, the late Charlie "Sourdough" Carson, had other ideas about how to go snow camping, and they are certainly worth describing here. After he retired from working on the Alaska Railroad, Charlie spent his winters trapping and taking friends

Author carries overnight camp on his back, using a summertime nylon rucksack. The whole load weighs less than 30 pounds.

on cross-country snowshoe trips to share his excess enthusiasm. A number of scout troops were invited to go on these winter expeditions, and they were surely fortunate for the experience. Charlie also enjoyed taking out military personnel stationed at Elmendorf and Fort Richardson where he became well known as an unofficial adviser on winter survival.

But Charlie had one unwavering theory. "Men wasn't designed," he would tell anyone, "to carry loads on their backs. That's for animals. I know better ways."

One of his better ways was to load everything on a light sled or toboggan and drag it behind him. That's how he could take a modestly comfortable camp instead of bare essentials along on every trip. A sled loaded with 100 pounds of gear, say, can soon become a chore for one man on snowshoes. But if the job is rotated regularly among all in the party, it's not hard on anyone,

If you're on snowshoes and don't mind pulling a sled, you can have a truly comfortable snow camp, including even a gasoline lantern, which provides heat as well as warmth.

The igloo is the most sophisticated form of snow shelter.

especially when the sled hauler walks last over a trail broken and compacted by the others.

Whenever possible, Charlie would shun artificial shelters. If late in the season and the winter's snow was hard packed, he would build an igloo, which really isn't a complicated task. The technique is to cut or saw out blocks of fairly uniform, 12- to 15-inch square cubes of snow. Arrange the first cubes—blocks—in a complete circle about eight feet in diameter on a stomped-out, flat area of snow. On top of these lay (as in laying bricks or concrete blocks) a second circle of snow blocks, but this time with the circle having a smaller diameter. Continue building upward, always decreasing the circle diameter to form a beehive-shaped structure. Cut out a small, low entrance on one side and build a small barrier around it to cut off wind. The body heat of several occupants and a small cooking fire will keep it warm inside and will soon, in fact, seal off any cracks or flaws in the construction as the blocks settle firmly into place.

If you can find the right spot, it is easier and faster to build a snow or ice cave. First step is to locate a drift or accumulation of snow deep enough that a living space or burrow can be excavated down and underneath it. To accommodate one or two persons (but snow caves can be dug to hold many more), first dig an entranceway back and down into the snow or snowbank. Then, on a level above that, but farther back, excavate (with a small light infantry or trenching shovel) a chamber or cubicle big enough for one or two (say six feet by four feet by four feet high) to either stretch out on sleeping bags or sit upright while cooking a meal. The more room to unwind, the better.

The reason for the down-and-then-up-again-entrance is to keep wind from blowing directly in. If done properly, the cave will be warm while temperatures are very low outside. If you were chilled when you started digging the snow cave, you will certainly be warm again when it's time to settle down inside.

Obviously a cave site must be selected with care. Any potential avalanche or steep sloping areas should be avoided because a snow slide could cover up the entrance and entomb the campers inside. Look instead for fairly level spots where the snow is stable and has had time to be well compacted.

Camping via snowshoes or touring skis isn't a game to be taken lightly or without sound planning; that point cannot be emphasized enough. Nor is it wise to wander off alone without built-up experience or training. Better to go in the beginning with an experienced guide and mentor. Incidentally, professional training is possible on a classroom-plus-field-trip basis. Some colleges in the Rocky Mountains offer courses in winter/mountain camping. Van Tribble, who teaches a winter adult education course in ski camping at Jackson, Wyoming, high school, has as many students enrolled as he can handle. They are equally divided, male and female, and range in age from 18 to 62. No generation gap there, and dropouts from the course are unknown.

Above: Cross-country skiing guide/instructor Van Tribble digs into a drift to hollow out an overnight ice cave. He uses a collapsible infantry trenching shovel to dig an under-snow chamber with a lower entranceway to the outside. *Opposite:* The cave finished, Tribble waxes skis in the entrance.

Now for a slightly unpleasant word in an otherwise happy discussion. Unlike so many snowmobilers, who leave a trail of litter, of raucous sound and exhaust behind them, most skiers and snowshoers are normally neat, fastidious, and concerned about the environment. But we have noted an exception that has to do with campers, and this is probably the place to insert it.

There is a tendency to relax when faraway in a winter woods— to neglect housekeeping—probably because it seems that the next snow will cover forever any wastes that are discarded. But we have found snow camps in springtime that looked like miniature hobo jungles. No amount of new snow could keep the litter from "blossoming" again when April rolled around. It shouldn't be that way. So leave nothing behind you except the ski or webbed tracks that lead into a lovely white distance.

9

Wildlife Watching and Photography

On a cold and glittering afternoon in January, with the temperature hovering at 15 above, Peggy and I began a now commonplace winter adventure. With a new wax coating on our skis, our rucksacks loaded with cameras, extra lenses, film, high-calorie snacks, and a few emergency items, we glided quietly across the immensely beautiful, snow-covered valley of Jackson Hole. Through dark wraparound sunglasses we carefully scanned the landscape ahead and all around us.

For a short distance we paralleled the Gros Ventre River which passes near our doorstep but which now was almost frozen solid. We crossed at a safe place and on the opposite side immediately came upon the familiar tracks of a coyote. The paw prints were so fresh that I suspected the coyote had been watching us make the crossing.

"Let's follow," I suggested, "and see what it's up to."

We spent most of that afternoon leisurely pursuing one of America's most fascinating animals as it wandered in search of subsistence. Once we even skied just close enough to shoot several photos with a telephoto lens at long range. These pictures were not especially good ones because of the great distance, plus my own unsteadiness, but it is remarkable that the coyote allowed us to approach even close enough to see it at all. In this area surrounding Grand Teton National Park and the National Elk Refuge, coyotes

One day during a ski tour we found this bull moose waiting out a blizzard. Even when completely covered by snow, the animal remained in its bed.

are not constantly harassed as they are elsewhere by sheep ranchers, and so are more visible. But back to our adventure.

The coyote appeared to be hunting mice over the snow-crusted sagebrush flats, but if it caught any this afternoon, we found no evidence of it. No hair, no tiny droplets of blood. Twice it passed fairly close to livestock which paid absolutely no attention to it and vice versa. But most interesting of all was when the animal traveled directly beneath a band of seven mule deer bedded in sunshine on an open slope.

The coyote's passage did not even cause any to stand up and take particular notice. But our *own* approach close behind caused all to spook completely out of sight. That revealing incident—that

Skiers in eastern woodlands are likely to encounter whitetail deer or their tracks, but seldom a huge buck like this.

glimpse of a much maligned wild animal—alone made that exhilarating afternoon a most memorable experience. As a bonus on the way home, a cow and calf moose posed for close-up portraits while nibbling on tender red willow tips. Neither showed the slightest alarm at all at the clicking camera.

But let me make one point clear. That was not at all an unusual afternoon and in fact was typical. During the past few winters we have enjoyed many similar intimate encounters with wildlife, so easily that some are worth describing here. I also feel that, at least to some extent, skiers and snowshoers anywhere can have similar rewarding experiences at an otherwise dull time of year, wherever winter snows blanket the outdoors. Now let's examine the details.

Later on I describe how Peggy and I used snowshoes to reach excellent angling which is all but overlooked in the Rocky Mountain West. At the same time we discovered that snowshoes could also carry us closer to the wildlife of this region—near enough to take the pictures you see on these pages. In other words we could keep hunting all winter long with a camera.

We were not bothered with closed seasons, opening days, or bag limits. We could bag both big and small game, endangered species as well as common ones, all with a clean conscience and no powder burned. So can anyone else. The solution is in being mobile—in being able to travel across heavy snow, no matter how deep it drifts. There are two means available, of course: snowshoes and cross-country skis.

The way to go hunting with a camera is just to start out across country looking for targets. Naturally some areas such as parks, sanctuaries, and refuges are much better than others, and eventually these become easier and easier to locate—just as a gun hunter soon recognizes good pheasant cover or likely whitetail deer habitat. If we do not know an area well, or are exploring in a new place, we begin, whenever possible, by following waterways or drainages where cover is likely to be heavy.

As any veteran outdoorsman realizes, there is much to be learned from the signs etched in snow. A multitude of fresh tracks means animals nearby and these can be followed to a conclusion. Concentrate especially after a new snowfall. But tracks are not the only signs. Watch also where willows, balsam, alder, or other browse plants have been used. Droppings also tell a story of occupancy.

Weather, too, can play an important role. When it is very windy, raw, or blustery, we follow trails into timbered areas looking for both our own comfort and the wildlife we hope will be using the same shelter. On very still, very cold days, we seek out the numerous small ponds and brooks kept open here by warm springs and other thermal activity. Waterfowl can be expected to be concentrated in such sites, but a surprising amount of other wildlife collects here too. That is surely the situation in Yellowstone where most of that national park's wintering species can be seen at close range around warm springs areas from December through March.

Wildlife almost anywhere behaves much differently in winter than at any other time of year and that isn't any wonder. Bitter cold and diminishing food supplies sap energy and animals do not move about as much or as readily. Game also seems to realize that this is not a hunting season. It follows that wildlife should not be tormented or harassed in any way. Whenever we suspected that a photo target resented our approaching any closer for pictures, we

Attempting to get through a fence, this elk was accidentally snared. But we found a coyote making good use of the carcass.

paused. It has cost some good exposures, but may also have made winter survival a little less trying for our targets.

I have read a good many articles on wildlife photography, and the consensus of advice is to use the same trophy tactics (be stealthy and stay hidden from the game) of gun hunting to get the best pictures when camera hunting. But that just isn't true.

From our own experiences skiing and snowshoeing, it is far better to make every effort to always stay in full view of whatever the photo target. Assume you have just spotted something—an elk, a buffalo, an owl, or whatever. Your best bet is to approach obliquely (*never* directly), very slowly, keeping the camera focused and ready to shoot, without making sudden moves or sounds, without ever staring very long or very directly at the creature. Stop often and do not "push" an animal. Make an effort to seem

Speaking of unusual encounters, how about this one of three, not two, bull moose sparring in a forest opening near a ski trail?

disinterested and to resemble just another critter trying to stay alive during difficult times. Nearly all subjects will be far less wary of a stranger they can keep an eye on than one who tries to stalk, surprise, or sneak up on them.

Last winter we located a great gray owl, largest of our native owls, rather rare anywhere and certainly not a commonly encountered bird. I desperately wanted pictures of this owl and so determined to use my own best advice.

The bird was perched in an aspen only about 20 feet above the ground. That was handy. But the tree was well up a very steep slope; climbing it with snowshoes was a backbuster, but impossible without them because the snow was four feet deep. The altitude was about 7000 feet above sea level and that explains why I was puffing when barely underway uphill.

My strategy was to approach a couple of steps at a time while never going directly toward the tree, circling and pausing for an exposure at each stop. But most of the early, more distant exposures were wasted because I was eventually able to reach within 12 feet on an even face-to-face level! Only then did the owl stretch, blink its cold yellow eyes at me, and fly away. I'm convinced the big bird behaved so well because it was never surprised and had me under surveillance all the time.

But as I said, wildlife is normally much tamer in winter. Most of my earlier experiences with ruffed grouse have been brief, with the bird disappearing swiftly and noisily into the nearest tangle. But last winter my problem was reversed. We located the birds by their telltale chickenlike tracks bisecting our own. But instead of flushing, many crouched in easy camera range—except too often in dark green shadows of evergreens too dark for filming. When they did decide to move away from us, most of the birds flushed quietly, never really exploded in typical grouse style.

Often sage grouse were even more cooperative; many we encountered neither flushed wildly nor hid in deep shadows. They kept a safe distance, but one not out of the range of a telephoto lens. Incidentally, we often found places where coyotes tried to capture sage hens, but none successfully. These escapes were clearly engraved in the snow.

We've used a number of different cameras for this snowshoe photography, but the 35 millimeter single lens reflex is certainly

Magnificent animals like these bull elk are seen frequently by skiers and snowshoers headquartered at Snow Lodge, Yellowstone, throughout the winter.

the best for the purpose. It is the lightest, most compact, and fastest to use on frequently unpredictable and often moving targets. My own camera happens to be equipped with a motor drive for shooting sequences and concentrating on the subject without being distracted by having to advance film.

A telephoto lens is also a necessity because, even under the most favorable conditions, it is rarely possible to get close enough with a normal (50 millimeters is normal for the 35 millimeter camera) lens. I have used telephotos as long as 500 millimeters (or 10 power), but most of the time this is too cumbersome to hand-hold steadily, and lugging a tripod is not practical. It is far better to be patient, cautious, and to approach close enough to use a 200 millimeter (4 power) or 300 millimeter (6 power) telephoto at the most. My favorite for winter shooting on skis is a 200. Unless any

Another large animal found coping with Yellowstone's deep snows is the bison. We came upon this one while skiing along the Firehole River.

telephoto is held completely still, blurred pictures result, a problem that can be solved by lugging a light monopod, using it also as a ski pole. Much more detail on equipment is contained in my own book, *Hunting with a Camera*, also published by Winchester Press.

Without question the handiest, most cooperative and dependable of our photo subjects are the several moose which spend the winters within easy skiing distance of our home. It's seldom any trouble to find one or maybe even several to pose, and we've become extremely attached to them. It is always very sad, therefore, to find them thin, emaciated, and weakened toward the end of a long, brutal winter. Not all, in fact, survive—and neither do all of the deer that headquarter near us. From time to time we can locate a carcass from the noisy, encircling ravens which soon gather on the scene. Then, by frequently visiting the spot, it is possible to shoot not only the scavenging ravens and magpies, but the coyotes

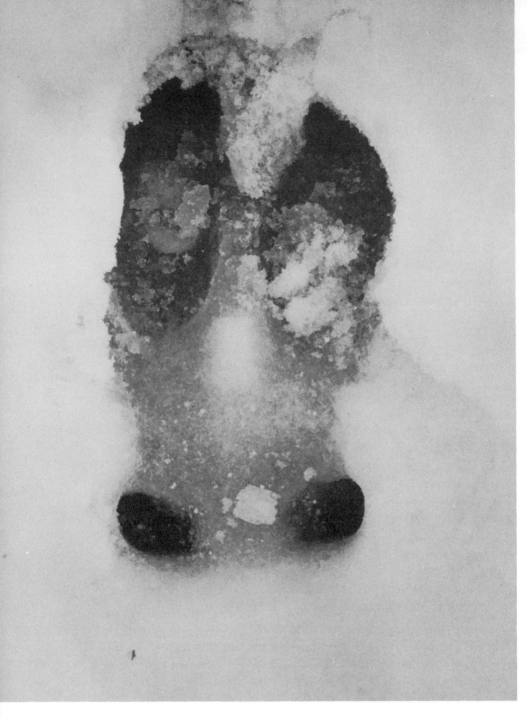

When touring across the quiet world always watch for wildlife tracks. This one was made by a moose.

as well. The latter make so much use of natural winter kills that it seems to be the only way the wild dogs can survive.

It is obvious enough that wildlife does not exist everywhere—or even anywhere—in such numbers as in Jackson Hole and in such situations that it can be hunted easily with a camera. Too much of our wild land has been plowed under or despoiled. But there are opportunities, and some very similar, everywhere that the American landscape is locked up under deep snows. It is only a matter of going out and finding them. And as I mentioned before, start out in the numerous parks and refuges.

Not all of our days afield have produced pictures suitable for publication; some, in fact, have been total blanks. But we rarely failed to find tracks that told interesting tales, even if we did not spot the track-makers themselves. And that is not the half of it.

Just being out in a winter woods on dazzlingly bright days as well as during snow squalls is a refreshing escape, a high adventure. It is an excellent means of "learning" an unfamiliar woods, of gaining much confidence about being in wilderness, a confidence that comes only with experience. Confidence, to tell the truth, can make you a better woodsman, a keener observer. Regular outings for wildlife will certainly keep your legs and lungs, your whole body, in much better physical shape without the drudgery of exercising at home or in a gym. There is always so much to fascinate.

Toward the tag end of last winter, longer days and receding snows eventually made us store away the webs and the skis until another season. It was a sad occasion made bittersweet by the fine picture trophies we'd collected. But I couldn't forget the countless, glorious days when we left behind the first and only human tracks across a cold white landscape. *Those* were the days, my friends.

10

Fishing and Hunting

As I NOTED in the first chapter, one of the best investments in fishing gear I ever made was the money I forked out for two pairs of trapper snowshoes. The $70 seemed extravagant then for something that a person couldn't even cast. But the money went toward the greatest off-season fishing I've ever found anywhere—and it cured a terrible case of cabin fever.

It all started on a blindingly bright afternoon in March when Peggy and I were driving some back roads, looking for wildlife to photograph. But both of us completely forgot about taking photographs the instant we crossed one highway bridge over the Snake River.

A short distance downstream, many fish were dimpling the surface of the water. Despite the wintry landscape, the scene resembled the rising of trout to an insect hatch that you might encounter only in midsummer. No wonder we had a hard time believing our own eyes.

For a few moments we just watched in amazement as the steady rises continued. Then I grabbed the fly rod that always rides in the back of my four-wheel-drive station wagon. I quickly rigged up the outfits, but the effort was wasted. The feeding fish might just as well have been on another planet instead of only 30 yards away, because I couldn't reach the water's edge to get within casting distance of the fish. Instead, I floundered helplessly in a waist-deep snowdrift. I became thoroughly chilled, and Peggy and I soon headed home to thaw out.

Later that evening Peggy seemed to be reading my mind as I thought about the rise on the river.

"Why not get a pair of snowshoes?" she asked. "Or better still—*two* pairs."

Early the next morning we drove to town and bought the webs. We had taken the first step toward finding a great new way to beat the winter doldrums with a brand of angling that's guaranteed to warm up anybody's winter. And other sportsmen who live in or near the northern Rocky Mountains, the Pacific Northwest, or southwestern Canada can do the same.

The next day we went back to the bridge over the Snake. We donned light thigh-high rubber boots and the new snowshoes, and it was suddenly amazingly easy to reach the water. From that one deep green pool just below the bridge, we caught an even dozen whitefish weighing one to two and a half pounds apiece. Our total catch weighed 18 pounds. For us that trip may have been the most exciting day of the entire year; it was also a revelation.

Some outdoorsmen may not think catching a big string of whitefish is a big deal, but they're missing a lot. There is no reason to apologize for catching whites, which are every bit as game as any trout of the same size. And besides, any species that can stretch out the angling season by two or three months is valuable as far as I'm concerned.

If the mountain whitefish has a shortcoming, it is simply that the species is too easy to catch and too abundant. It is a salmonid and therefore is a relative of all North American salmon, trout, chars, grayling, and sheefish. In some waters whites have become superabundant, and many anglers consider them a nuisance, if not a trash fish. Some fisheries biologists share that view; because of the whitefish's greater reproductive potential and other characteristics, they suspect that the whitefish may be a serious competitor of trout.

But culprit or not, the whitefish is here to stay, and the best way to correct any imbalance with trout is to harvest as many whitefish as possible. Wyoming has a generous daily limit of 25 whitefish per day (and 75 in possession). Other states also have liberal regulations. If you can find deep holes where whitefish concentrate or "layer-up" in winter, it isn't hard to catch a limit—and it certainly can be exciting.

On another cold, sunny day late in March, Peggy and I drove north from home toward the south entrance of Yellowstone (that's as far as the highway is kept open until the spring thaw begins in May). At that point it is a walk of only a few hundred yards over three- to four-foot snowbanks to the Snake. The hike was easy for us with our new snowshoes.

Near the tail of one deep pool we found a few fish feeding on top, apparently on tiny gnat-sized midges that hatch in winter and are often called snowflies. I rigged up an 8½-foot medium trout-weight fly rod (a lighter outfit might be even better) with a tapered line and a 12-foot tapered 4X leader. I tied on a snowfly imitation. Then I waded out and began casting upstream and across toward the risers.

"Get the camera," I said to Peggy, "and be ready for some action."

But the only action was fruitless casting. I changed to smaller patterns and to other colors of snowflies, but that didn't help. Nor did changing over to nymphs. Finally I waded back to shore where Peggy had built a small fire. I changed reels to one that had a sinking line. Then I put on a fresh leader and knotted it to a No. 12 muskrat-fur nymph.

Halfway through the drift of my first cast, a whitefish inhaled the nymph and my fly rod was dancing. The fish made a short run across the current, then turned downstream and into a riffle. I beached the 13-incher a few moments later and cached it in the nearest snowbank. On each of my next six casts I hooked whitefish. When 11 fish were in the snowbank the action stopped and we had to search downstream for another deep pool. But the snowshoes made it easy for us. Less than a quarter-mile away we found a spot where whitefish were as willing as they'd been in the first pool. Soon we had the legal limits.

The most commonly used rig is a spinning outfit with a one-quarter- to one-half-ounce sinker on the end of six- or eight-pound test monofilament line. A plastic bubble or bobber is set at a distance up the line equal to the depth of the pool. A dropper line is then knotted to the line near the sinker. The dropper is baited with a grub or mealworm of the type used by icefishermen. The bait is cast upstream and allowed to drift back down through the pool, bumping along the bottom. This is a deadly way to catch plenty of whitefish, but I prefer the sport and challenge of taking the fish on flies and a light fly rod.

Throughout the winter, weighted nymphs are the flyfisherman's best bets for whitefish. On the Snake some other hot patterns are George's Brown Stone Nymph, Whit Golden Nymph, Whit Bronze Nymph, Hare's Ear Nymph, and Quill Gordon Nymph. For some reason snowfly imitations (fished either wet or dry) are more effective than nymphs on certain rivers—most notably on the Yellowstone in Montana. Even when whitefish are rising very actively to naturals, they will often shun even the best-presented dries in favor of any nymph that's drifted close to the bottom. These are exasperating situations that I can't explain. The important thing to remember, however, is that whitefish will always eagerly take *something*.

But our whitefishing adventures have involved more than just the exciting, overlooked sport. Although we rarely ran into other humans, we did meet other "fishermen" such as families of otters and a number of bald eagles. We often saw moose that were wintering in the willow bottoms. We saw numerous Barrow's goldeneyes. And we even caught occasional glimpses of rare trumpeter swans and of strange water ouzels.

Another bonus of winter whitefishing is that this species is delicious on the table. I don't think trout or any other fish living within the whitefish range is nearly as good.

It is legal and possible to catch enough whitefish to justify fueling and operating a smoker, and most fishermen prefer to smoke their catches. Smoking is easy to do at home, and smoked whitefish is a great delicacy.

The first step is to field-dress the fish, leaving them whole. Marinate them overnight in a heavy brine solution that's strong enough to float an egg. Next, place the fish on trays in a smoker (the smoker can be a manufactured model or simply an old 50-gallon drum, an old refrigerator, or a small brick or concrete-block kiln) for 12 to 15 hours. Use hardwood for the fire. Regulate the fire as much as possible to produce steady smoke rather than heat. This may require a good bit of manipulating, but the results are certainly worthwhile. The addition of green willow shoots will partly smother a fire, causing "cold" smoke. Smoked whitefish makes an excellent, highly nutritious snack when ski-touring or snowshoeing anytime.

The sporty and good-tasting whitefish is just one of several species available to the skiing or snowshoeing angler.

Fried whitefish is equally good, and is even easier to prepare than smoked whitefish. Dress the fish, and cut off heads and tails. Peel off the skin with pliers. This is quite easy to do if the fish is fresh; later on (especially if the fish have been frozen) it is a little harder. Larger fish should be cut into sections.

Wipe the pieces completely dry, and dip each one into beaten egg and then into a mixture of pancake flour, cracker crumbs, garlic salt, and coarse pepper. Allow the dipped fish to sit for a few minutes while you heat some peanut oil that's about one inch deep in a high iron skillet or Dutch oven to 370–400 degrees. Cook the fish in this hot oil for four or five minutes or until it's golden and crisp on the outside. The inside will then be white, moist flakes. You can serve it with hot cornbread and a salad of the watercress that grows wild in many spring-fed streams throughout whitefish country.

The whitefish's range includes all the region from the west slope of the Rockies to the Pacific Ocean, from northern California and Utah north to British Columbia. The fish is also native to head-waters of the Yellowstone, Missouri, and those Saskatchewan rivers that do not drain into the Pacific. Although the whitefish generally prefers rivers, it is also found in Lakes Tahoe, Donner, Independence, and Upper and Lower Twin in the High Sierra. All of this is also superb ski-touring and snowshoeing country.

Besides those streams I've already mentioned, a list of excellent whitefish rivers would include Utah's Logan, the Truckee, Carson, and Walker river systems on the east slope of the Sierra; the Missouri, Jefferson, Madison, and Gallatin in Montana; the Silver Creek and the Snake and Salmon rivers in Idaho. The fish's main requirement seems to be stretches of cold, pure water at least three feet deep—water that's also the home of sculpins, suckers, and other minnows as well as all species of trout and steelhead.

But there is far more than just whitefishing to encourage a sportsman to buy skis or snowshoes. Official creel censuses made in many northern states from Maine to Montana have revealed that angling actually is best after summertime fishermen go home and particularly after a crust of ice covers many lakes. In other words, success (per time spent fishing) through the ice is much higher than during the normal fishing season. At the same time, winter fishing pressure is very light because there are many ice-locked lakes that not even snowmobiles can reach. The lesson here is that a person on skis or snowshoes can have a good bit of excellent and exclusive fishing all winter long. It may just be a matter of going out on winter weekends, tackle in a rucksack, and staking a claim.

Skis can greatly reduce the time required to reach a fishing hole far out on the ice.

I am not going to reveal the location of one small bonanza we discovered last winter, except to say that it is less than two miles from a busy highway in summertime and for the most part accessible over a fairly gentle hiking trail. Don't bother to look for it on any maps because Beaver Pond is not the correct name for it. However, beavers were responsible for "building" this fishing hole which is a dam woven across the outlet of a natural lake to increase the depth enough that both cutthroat and brook trout could be stocked.

Finding Beaver Pond was a dividend of a short afternoon snowshoe jaunt during a snow squall, mostly just for the exercise. We followed a trail familiar to summer hikers for about a mile and then turned to examine the fresh tracks of a cow and calf moose. We followed these for a distance across a frozen bog where the going was tough because our webbing became entangled in clumps of willow which protruded above the ice. But beyond that it was clear and we came upon the two moose, both bedded down, the black bodies covered with snow. I shot several photos of the huge animals, and we turned to head homeward again. The snow was falling harder.

"But isn't that an opening just ahead?" Peggy said, "It even looks like a lake."

"Let's push on and see," I answered without enthusiasm.

That's how we happened to find Beaver Pond. And at the same time we almost forgot it in our hurry to be away. But a week or so later, as I wound monofilament line onto our ice-fishing reels, Peggy wondered if it wouldn't be worth visiting again. Next morning we did, only this time carrying our ice tackle, tiny ice flies, and jigs, a small auger for cutting holes, and no great optimism.

What followed wasn't as thrilling, say, as flycasting through deep blue pools where the schools of whitefish lurk. Ice-fishing seldom is that way. But under the gradually penetrating sun of a still February day, we fooled enough trout for the most delicious dinner of the whole season. Except for a few Oregon juncos and a Clark's nutcracker that came to inspect our interloping, we had Beaver Pond and the quiet wilderness surrounding it entirely to ourselves.

That day alone was a good excuse for investing in skis and snowshoes. And there were countless others.

Snowshoes made it possible to reach this remote and lonely lake in northern Michigan where ice fishing pays off.

Snowshoes can play an important part when hunting snowshoe hares late in the season all across the northern U.S. and southern Canada.

Hiking in the winter woods is a good way to find foxes and to run a trapline.

Then there is also the matter of hunting. Almost invariably some of the finest trophy bucks and bulls are bagged just as hunting seasons come to an end; at least the later in the season the better the odds for a bragging-size set of horns. There is a good explanation for this. In most of the mountainous West, deer and elk tend to stay as high as possible and migrate downward toward winter ranges only when foul weather and deep snows drive them. Not always, but often, they reach low, accessible (to hunters) elevations just before the legal season ends. So anyone who can brave the elements to be afield has a fine chance of scoring.

But take our word that hunting is no pleasure, no easy matter at all, when a foot of snow covers the ground. The best-conditioned man soon flounders and gets tired, even though the white cover does expose his target more and give him an advantage. This then is where skis or snowshoes come in handy. One or the other can change a dismal hunt into a successful one.

In some areas, skis or webs are just the ticket for such other winter hunting as foxes, coyotes, jackrabbits, or snowshoe hares. Open seasons exist on all of these in snow country. A wintertime trapper can also at least double his range or cover his trapline far more quickly if he can travel swiftly over the snow rather than slog through it.

One friend of ours, Pete Flambeau, who annually traps a vast northern muskrat marsh, actually doubled his catch beginning the first winter he used snowshoes. With the increased profits he bought a pair of cross-country skis and now runs the entire trapline in still less time.

"Next season," he joked in a thick French accent, "I buy me a pair of those red gaiters, too, and maybe a fancy colored shirt. A trapper in my position has to dress for it. Now that I'm on skis, I have to look like all those skiers in the catalogs."

Well, not exactly. But thanks to the advantage of the skis, the old trapper can at last afford it.

Whether hunting with a gun, bow, or camera, following a deer track across a snowy landscape can be a fascinating sport.

11

Coping with Common Winter Emergencies

ALMOST NO MATTER WHEN OR WHERE a human ventures outdoors, he is likely to encounter dangers. That's part of the game. And the farther he travels from "civilization" the greater the risks he faces. Escape to nature is a great thing—one of the most priceless dividends of the outdoors—but it can also be a test or even an exercise in survival. In some places the outdoorsman must cope with intense heat and humidity; elsewhere, on deserts, the scarcity of water may be the main concern. For skiers and snowshoers, intense cold and exposure are the problems.

As strange as it may seem, many emergencies occur or are caused before a skier or snowshoer ever tightens the bindings on his boots or waxes his skis. Just getting into and out of skiing areas by car can cause problems. Let's try here to anticipate some of them.

Say you live in a latitude where the sun is shining and you plan to aim north to enjoy a bit of *real* winter. Well, bravo. But before heading northward, you had better be sure that your car is up to it. How about the tires, for instance; is the tread suitable for snow going? If not, do you have chains you can install? And the radiator? Have you added the antifreeze necessary to see you through zero temperatures? Do you have a shovel, axe, tow chain, or rope? Most critical of all may be a battery that will get you started when the engine is stiff and cold. It takes a lot more battery power to start at zero than it does in balmy temperatures. Jumper cables (which anyone living in frigid winter country should always carry) will help some other motorist to get you started. But what if you happen to be alone somewhere?

When planning your trip, allow for plenty of time to go slowly. Listen to radio and state highway patrol advisories, and keep advised of road conditions and any bad storms expected. It takes a little time to get safely acquainted with driving on snow and ice, a task which is magnified by mountainous country.

Okay, you have now reached the skiing area, and up ahead a ski trail meanders off into the forest. But don't just park your car in any old place. Instead face it toward home while the motor is still warm. It is very important to have clear, solid, unobstructed going when you want to leave a place. Don't set the handbrake; it could freeze. Use low gear instead and maybe a log wedged under the rear wheels. If you have one of those pickups or other vehicles in which the battery is exposed or located under the floor boards, check to see that no slush has accumulated on top of the terminals. This will soon freeze in place and furnish just enough conductivity to run down even a brand new battery.

Do not carry the car keys in your pocket as you head across country; the chances of losing them are too great. Rather, hide them in some place that every member of the party knows about. Many skiers also leave notes attached to the windshield, which state when and where the party went, and when they expect to be back. It is excellent free insurance of which passing rangers or patrolmen will take note.

In extremely low, sub-zero situations, especially for lengthy periods, it will pay to have an engine block heater installed. These can be plugged overnight into 110 volt outlets. The cost of heater and installation is about $35–$40. Otherwise drain the oil every night and remove the battery, keeping both in a warm shelter.

Be careful when refueling with gasoline, both because of its flammability and to avoid freezing your hands. Liquid gasoline can get much colder than the freezing point of water, and a lot of it on exposed skin can cause severe, painful blistering.

Now you are ready to hit the trail, convinced that all is okay with your car. This is the time you have been waiting for.

The essence of coping with winter—or staying safe and comfortable on the trail—is wisely conserving your body heat and energy. Strive to maintain heat, as we've urged before, and not

Few skiers will ever have to worry about survival under dire circumstances, but you should plan carefully before heading out on any major cross-country trips.

overheat. Do not push yourself unduly, especially if you are not certain of your own capacity. If you are part of a party, travel at a steady pace that the slowest person can maintain without struggling. Chances are that it will also be a good pace for all.

Avoid any iron-man acts. When breaking a new trail or traveling over an old one which is snow-drifted, alternate the leaders. If anybody's boots begin to rub or pinch, if bindings need adjustment, stop and correct the cause immediately. Folds of a sock, too-tight laces or straps, or nails can be very irritating. Bandage or tape any scraped, red, or raw spots on the skin. If the going still seems burdensome for anyone, it may be that the skis are not properly waxed. Correct this and you may also solve uncomfortable foot or boot problems. Don't allow yourself or anyone to sweat. Keep your clothing dry. Add on foul-weather gear *before* you need it.

Never travel farther than you can also travel back easily, and do not be ashamed that during any snowshoe or ski tour it may be necessary to turn back earlier than planned. After all, you're out skiing for fun, not to invite an ordeal. Keep an eye on the weather, which may change swiftly; deteriorating weather could create problems in getting back to a starting point. Low sweeping clouds can obscure landmarks on which you depended and the wind which accompanies storms can steal the body heat you need.

Without a doubt most accidents occur on return trips, when skiers are tired, hungry, perhaps wet or cold. The inclination is to take shortcuts, to tackle steeper hills than is wise, to try unfamiliar trails to gain time. Resist all these temptations. Above all, and we repeat because it cannot be overemphasized, keep warm, avoid perspiration, and keep clothing dry.

Heat loss can occur in many ways—by radiation, conduction, convection, evaporation, respiration, wind chill, and water chill. Let's try to translate all of these into more understandable language.

In most recreational ski-touring, radiation is the chief cause of heat loss. Not wearing a cap can cause you to lose up to 50 percent of your body's total heat at 40 degrees Fahrenheit. It is a fact that you can warm cold feet by putting on a hat. When you contact anything colder than your skin, you lose heat through conduction. So no matter how tired, don't sit or lie on the cold ground.

It's unwise to travel great distances or long hours on webs or skis, especially if you're alone. Before the sun begins to set, you should turn your thoughts and your tracks toward home.

The function of clothing, as stated before, is to retain a layer of radiated warm air close to the body in order to maintain the normal 98.6 degrees temperature. Convection—as cooler air passing the body—tends to remove the warm air. The faster the wind, or exchange of air, the greater the heat loss. Evaporation of sweat and a skier's breath dissipate warmth. So does respiration, or inhaling cold air. This can be reduced by breathing through a scarf or a mask made for that purpose.

When the wind increases, even moderate temperatures become more difficult to maintain. That means adding more clothing or providing other shelter for the body. Water chill is worse, as evidenced by the fact that wet clothing can extract heat from the body many, many times as fast as dry clothing. Wool, we reiterate, is warmer than other fabrics when wet. But keep wool dry, too.

It is as necessary to conserve energy as warmth; indeed the two depend on each other. Anybody's usable supply of energy is strictly limited; you can go only so far on a given intake. For example, to sustain life for 24 hours it requires about 1700 calories with the body at rest at a comfortable temperature. But ski-touring can expend 5000 to 6000 calories per day and even more, depending on how cold the weather and how rough the terrain. Strenuous exercise uses up these calories rapidly as they also produce heat— so of course the calories must be replaced.

Besides eating a nourishing and well-balanced diet while on a skiing or snowshoeing schedule, a skier should always carry along a supply of high-energy foods to replace lost calories (energy). While pausing at intervals not to exceed five minutes or so at a time (a five-minute break will get rid of 30 percent of the lactic acid build-up in muscles, which comes from hard exertion, but little lactic acid is eliminated after that), enjoy a welcome snack.

Fortunately the same high-calorie foods which are best for this purpose are also the most delicious: raw brown sugar, chocolate, chocolate, chocolate, any kind of salted nuts, from pecans to cashews, dried fruit, honey, or maple syrup concentrated to sugar. Various mixtures of these things are called gorp and sold in ski or mountain shops. But anyone can make his own favorite formula less expensively. One of the things Peggy likes best about ski-touring is that she can eat *all* of the chocolate she likes, while at the same time keeping in the most beautiful trim.

"It's eating your cake," she admits, "and having it, too."

An active ski tourer or snowshoer needs a good intake of water daily to replace moisture lost through perspiration, breathing, and urination. If very active, three or four quarts may not be too much to prevent dehydration. Salt in the gorp (or as tablets) will help retain water longer, but there is some disagreement about the value of this salt supplement. Anyway, drink plenty of water before starting out on a tour and also at the end of it. Many veteran skiers train to get along without drinking during a trip, and absolutely avoid the temptation of eating snow because that may make thirst seem worse. If you must have water on a trip and all surface sources are frozen, carry a supply in a canteen. It is not advisable to carry or drink alcoholic beverages—not even light wine—when far out in a cold winter woods. Any stimulation from it will be false at best and deadly at worst, so save the imbibing for celebrating at the end of the day.

Getting lost is a possibility which must be considered, and every traveler over snow should be mentally prepared to cope with it. Assume you have lost the trail and your bearings. You do not know exactly where you are. The very first thing is to stop, sit down in a dry spot, if possible, and think about it. Resist any kind of hasty action or panic. If there are several in the party, all should stay together and discuss the situation together. To act frantically—to get unhinged—is the worst thing that could possibly happen. Relax.

Even without a compass and map (which somebody should have carried), it is possible to determine general direction, as long as someone has a watch and even a weak sun is shining. Hold a match or straight twig upright at the edge of the watch. Turn the watch until the shadow of the stick falls directly along the hour hand, no matter what the hour. Halfway between the hour hand and the 12 points to due south. Exactly opposite is north.

If knowing the direction still doesn't help, if landmarks are non-existent, and particularly if it is getting late or dark, decide to camp in the most sheltered situation nearby. Put on all the clothing you have. Calmly, slowly, using as little energy as possible, collect as much firewood as is handy and then some. Pile it up where it will be handy. By all means, avoid sweating. Collect enough evergreen boughs for insulation to sit or lie down on—perhaps even

Besides being well stocked with survival equipment, a skier should be in top physical condition before beginning an ambitious adventure.

enough to make a lean-to shelter as a windbreak. Light the fire and keep it going, both to keep yourself warm and because the smoke will attract attention. Again, keep calm.

In a situation such as this, it's impossible not to experience apprehension and probably moments of great fear. Sure it's a tight spot, but probably one of discomfort more than danger. Be assured that nowadays there are sophisticated rescue facilities and professional patrols everywhere. Their record for finding people in the toughest spots is extraordinary.

Still—cold can kill, and to understand it is to prepare better to cope with it, as well as with the fatigue and exhaustion that go along with it.

When skiing or snowshoeing, the moment your body begins to lose heat faster than it produces heat, you are undergoing exposure. One of two things happens: Either you voluntarily exercise to stay warm, or your body makes involuntary adjustments to preserve normal temperature in the vital organs. Either response drains energy reserves. The only way to stop the drain is to reduce the degree of exposure.

If exposure continues until energy reserves are exhausted, cold reaches the brain as elsewhere. You begin to lose judgment, but do not realize it. You also begin to lose control of your hands, and internal temperature begins sliding downward. This condition is called hypothermia. With the body temperature falling to 90 degrees and below, the slide leads to stupor, collapse, and death.

But there are definite defenses against exposure and hypothermia. We have frequently pointed out the need to stay dry. You should also beware of the wind. Scientists of the World Health Organization now know that survival of Eskimoes was always made possible by the fact that they remained indoors, inactive, or both, during the periods of most severe wind. Instinctively, they avoided exposure.

So understand the true nature of cold. Curious as it may seem, most hypothermia cases develop in air temperatures between 30 and 50 degrees Fahrenheit with wind and wetness added. Many outdoorsmen simply cannot comprehend that such "moderate" temperatures are dangerous. In so doing, they fatally underestimate what can happen.

Summed up, if you cannot stay dry and warm under existing weather conditions using the clothing you have available, terminate exposure. Give up whatever goal you had in mind. Get out of the wind and rain the quickest possible way. Build a fire. Sit close to it. Calmly concentrate on making as comfortable a camp as possible.

Maybe you will be traveling in a party exposed to considerable wind, to cold and rain or wet snow. Then watch not only yourself but all others for symptoms of hypothermia such as uncontrollable fits of shivering, vague or slurred speech, memory lapses, fumbling hands, frequent stumbling, lurching gait, drowsiness, such advanced exhaustion as inability to get up after a rest. Any or all of these demand treatment. A victim may even deny that he's in trouble, but believe the symptoms, not the patient.

First get any victim out of wind and rain, indoors if possible. Strip off all wet clothes. If he is only mildly impaired, give the person warm, non-alcoholic drinks. Get him into dry clothes and a warm sleeping bag. Warm (but never hot) rocks wrapped in cloth, or a canteen of hot water, when slipped into the sleeping bag, will help.

If the victim is semi-conscious or worse, try to keep him awake, and supply warm drinks. Leave him stripped. Put him in a sleeping bag with another person who is in good shape, but also stripped. If you happen to have a double bag, put the person between two stripped persons. That skin to skin contact is a most effective treatment. But the main thing always is to prevent the onset of exhaustion and hypothermia. It is seldom difficult to do.

Each individual's tolerance to cold is different. And besides, there is a psychological factor, difficult to measure, involved. But the actual cold can be measured accurately by what is called a wind-chill factor. The U.S. military services have compiled the wind-chill chart on page 139 for anyone planning to be active outdoors in winter.

To use the chart, you need to know the temperature and wind force. Temperature can be read from a thermometer, but usually you must estimate wind force: calm—trees are motionless and smoke rises vertically; below 12 mph—smaller branches on trees move and you can feel the wind on exposed flesh; up to 24 mph—larger tree branches move and snow whirls over drifts; above 25 mph—largest branches and even tree trunks move, wind whistles, and walking into the wind is difficult. So is skiing.

Why not make the most of this chart before embarking on any long ambitious trips or when the weather prediction is not good? It could spare you much discomfort and save you for a sunnier day.

TEMPERATURE (degrees Fahrenheit)

EQUIVALENT CHILL TEMPERATURE

WIND MPH (miles per hour)	40	35	30	25	20	15	10	5	0	-5	-10	-15	-20	-25	-30	-35	-40	-45	-50	-55	-60
5	35	30	25	20	15	10	5	0	-5	-10	-15	-20	-25	-30	-35	-40	-45	-50	-55	-60	-70
10	30	20	15	10	5	0	-10	-15	-20	-25	-35	-40	-45	-50	-60	-65	-70	-75	-80	-90	-95
15	25	15	10	0	-5	-10	-20	-25	-30	-40	-45	-50	-60	-65	-70	-80	-85	-90	-100	-105	-110
20	20	10	5	0	-10	-15	-25	-30	-35	-45	-50	-60	-65	-75	-80	-85	-95	-100	-110	-115	-120
25	15	10	0	-5	-15	-20	-30	-35	-45	-50	-60	-65	-75	-80	-90	-95	-105	-110	-120	-125	-135
30	10	5	0	-10	-20	-25	-30	-40	-50	-55	-65	-70	-80	-85	-95	-100	-110	-115	-125	-130	-140
35	10	5	-5	-10	-20	-30	-35	-40	-50	-60	-65	-75	-80	-90	-100	-105	-115	-120	-130	-135	-145
40	10	0	-5	-15	-20	-30	-35	-45	-55	-60	-70	-75	-85	-95	-100	-110	-115	-125	-130	-140	-150

Winds above 40 mph have little additional effect

LITTLE DANGER

INCREASING DANGER
(flesh may freeze within one minute)

GREAT DANGER
(flesh may freeze within 30 seconds)

12

Avalanche!

SOMEONE RECALLS that the time was about 4 p.m. Wednesday, January 16, 1974, when Tom Warren led a party of strong young backpackers on skis across Glacier Gulch, which is about 9000 feet above sea level in Grand Teton National Park. It was the dead of winter—and cold. Warren was a veteran skier, climber, mountaineer, National Ski Patrolman, and an avalanche expert. The men following slowly in single file behind him were members of the National Outdoor Leadership School of Lander, Wyoming, which is headed by famed alpinist, Paul Petzholdt.

The group had traveled from Garnet Canyon over a ridge and into Glacier Gulch, most of that trip being within shelter of evergreen forest. Even beyond the timber was an area of giant rocks which seemed to anchor the deep snow and hold it in place. The skiers proceeded across the open space toward the base of Teton Glacier where they planned to dig a snow cave and spend the night. Darkness wasn't far away.

Then suddenly the whole world seemed to be moving, flowing downward.

The surge of the snow was silent and even dreamlike. At first most of the backpackers caught in it were perplexed rather than terrified. Then came a dreadful realization. Some started swimming—"treading water"—in the river of snow wider than a football field which moved inexorably down the slope.

"Swim!" a voice screamed, "Swim!" and that was the last sound some of them ever heard.

Pete Randall was swept aside to the lee side of a huge boulder where he remained until the avalanche stopped as quietly as it began. Luckily Wes Kraus managed to stay on top all the way by swimming. Don Webber was all but swallowed up in the slide, but when it was ended, managed to brush enough snow from his face with a free hand so that he could breathe. Nobody honestly recalls exactly what happened next, except that nine of the dozen were alive and three were missing.

With ski poles used as probes the three missing men were eventually located, dug out of entombment, and given mouth-to-mouth resuscitation. But it didn't work. Threatened by both darkness and further avalanching, the party had to give up the futile life-saving attempts and retreat to a safer place. In total black, Tom Warren and assistant instructor Bill Bruitigan plunged down the mountain to Park Headquarters at Moose with news of the tragedy. During that day and the next, other avalanches did occur throughout the Grand Teton range. They weren't unexpected.

There are a number of reasons for relating that awful and dramatic incident. Although avalanches are common in deep snow country every winter, they do claim surprising few lives of skiers, snowshoers, and others who are in the mountains. Although avalanche conditions are well known and are usually detectable, they do occur in unexpected or seemingly "safe" places. They are highly dangerous and destructive, ranking with floods, earthquakes, and volcanic eruptions as Nature's most destructive forces. But even when caught in terrible avalanches, it is possible to survive the experiences—and we will deal with all of these things in turn.

The same condition in recent winters which has helped our energy crisis by saving fuel—warm days following very cold nights—has also caused slides. "Wet" slides happen when a bright sun warms snow high in the mountains and permits water to seep through the piled-up snow. That breaks its adhesion to the ground. Then, without warning, the huge unglued mass can race down a slope at speeds greater than 60 miles per hour. Everything in the avalanche path is either crushed, buried, or both.

The so-called "dry" slides are triggered when storms deposit more snow than a mountain slope can hold in repose. These can spread destruction even faster and with more devastation than wet slides. Dry avalanches often exceed 100 miles per hour.

Avalanche records have been kept in alpine Europe for a long, long time because of their impact on winter life in mountain areas. One avalanche of dry snow in 1898, which hurtled down the Vorder-Glarnish region of eastern Switzerland, carried tens of thousands of tons of snow and debris for two miles down one side of a valley and part way up the opposite side. Today's avalanche researchers estimate that it must have reached a speed of 280 miles per hour.

Not only the rush of snow is destructive. An avalanche can force a column of compressed air ahead of it powerful enough to flatten all obstacles. In Austria several winters ago, the air pressure generated by a major snowslide blew freight cars off a railroad siding. Equally hazardous can be the vacuum in the wake of a giant slide. When an avalanche rushed over the village of Blons, Austria, in 1955, it created a vacuum which actually sucked people out of their homes.

Avalanches of dry snow can strike so swiftly—so savagely—that even when spotted there is little chance to get out of the way. Still—a good many victims "buried alive" have been able to breathe in air pockets (like miners trapped underground) and stay alive until rescue workers dug them free. There is a fairly well-known case (hard for this writer to swallow), for example, of a man in the Alps covered under tons of snow. He succeeded, it has often been reported, in getting himself out of entrapment by digging for ten days to reach the surface. Far more credible are the numerous reports of victims who survived after several hours under snow.

One rare type of avalanche, called "white death" in Europe, makes almost any escape impossible. It consists of masses of very light, powdery snow which fills the air like a cloud of deadly dust and sifts into the nose, eyes, and throat of anyone in the vicinity. People well away from the main slide path have still choked to death.

For the record, the worst avalanche disaster of recorded history happened on September 3, 1916, during World War I. Artillery barrages along the Austro-Italian front precipitated a whole series of slides which killed thousands of soldiers of both armies. During fighting in the Alps, it is believed there were more avalanche fatalities than deaths from either battle or influenza.

In January of 1962, an avalanche plunged from a glacier on

Nevado Huascarán in Peru's Andes Mountains and began a run down the 22,205-foot slope. Gathering speed, mud, and boulders along with the ice and snow, the forward edge of the avalanche was estimated to tower six stories high. In about seven minutes of horror, it wiped out eight villages and at least 3500 villagers. Almost all were covered forever.

North America has so far been spared such devastation, perhaps because we now know more about avalanches, what causes them, and even what prevents them. That includes, of course, even the smaller ones likely to threaten skiers or snowshoers out in the pursuit of recreation.

Avalanches are most likely to occur on slopes steeper than 25 degrees. The critical zone is from 35 degrees (a similar gradient to a staircase) and steeper, and therefore a zone to be avoided. Steep, unforested gullies are natural avalanche paths. So are strips already cleared by previous slides. Any unnatural scars on timbered slopes (such as clear-cut logging areas and downhill ski slopes, two commonly ignored examples) are apt to be avalanche paths, if steep. Heavily timbered slopes seldom slide. Steep southerly slopes favor avalanches after a fresh heavy snow and in late springtime.

Ideal avalanche weather and time is after a snowfall of 10 inches or more, and/or when snowfall exceeds an inch per hour, and/or there is a strong, perhaps warm wind of 12 mph or more. A very bad sign is fair weather with rapidly rising temperatures just after a heavy storm. Above freezing temperatures for 36 hours or so in spring promote deep thawing and wet avalanches. Rain has the same effect, except that it is even more serious.

Avalanche danger is therefore greatest after a large accumulation of new snow and for up to two days following such a storm. And any sun or rain on that snow which results in deep thawing is a likely trigger.

There are many obvious signs of avalanche danger, some apparently small and insignificant. Overhanging cornices of snow (which are very picturesque) may drop and cause snow on the slope below to begin sliding. Stay away from them. Be cautious when dry snow under skis sifts like sand into the ski track, rather than packing into a clean, sharp track. Watch out in steep places when damp snow slithers out from under skis or snowshoes and rolls away in balls or slips away in a layer. At the same time, sun-formed snowballs rolling away will probably be visible. Avoid wind-packed "slab" snow on steep mountainsides. This snow gives way suddenly, settles underfoot with a crunching sound. It may fracture into blocks and start an avalanche.

During most pleasure skiing and snowshoeing it is possible to avoid avalanches simply by staying clear of hazardous areas or even of doubtful areas—in other words by selecting safe routes. Take no unnecessary risks. Detour all known or suspected avalanche paths and slopes. This is surely the best advice of all.

But if for some reason—say to effect a rescue—avalanche terrain *must* be crossed, the early morning hours before sunup are the safest. In thawing weather, that period from mid-morning through sundown is the most dangerous. Travel south slopes whenever possible except in spring, when north is better. Travel is also relatively safe during the first few hours of a storm, but a traveler should hole up during a severe storm and wait until the new fall has had sufficient chance to slide or settle. Never ever cross any slopes where cracks open up out ahead of the skis.

When emergency or circumstance make it necessary to cross known avalanche terrain, the following is gospel: Loosen any pack so it can be discarded instantly; loosen ski or snowshoe bindings; take hands out of wrist loops on poles; pull up the parka hood and fasten across the face, leaving the eyes exposed. Cross the lower concave parts (as low as possible) of slopes, never the convex (bulged-by-snow or outward-curving) portions. It is fairly safe to proceed along the very crest of ridges. If in a party, one man should cross first, gliding to the far side. Then the second man, following the same path, and so on. But members should never go close together or roped one to another.

It is hoped that no readers of these words will ever be caught even in a small avalanche. But if you should somehow find yourself in a moving snowmass, ski or cross to the edge as quickly as possible and keep on going until well beyond it. On many snowslides that—amazingly—is possible.

If not—and to avoid being buried—get rid of skis, snowshoes, poles, and packs. Swim vigorously, lying on your back and with your feet downhill if you can manage it. Every effort must be made to stay on the surface and/or drift toward the edge. If that becomes impossible, try to keep your mouth and nose covered

Sharp drops like this one are prime potential-avalanche areas.

to avoid suffocation. When the slide stops, make the supreme effort to get as much air space as possible around your face and chest. Do it instantly, because a slide may quickly harden if the snow is at all wet.

Many avalanche victims have been rescued by prompt action from others. Remember and mark distinctly where a victim was last seen. Make a quick search of the slide path down along the fall line, below the last-seen point. Probe or dig around any piece of clothing or equipment you may find. Mark the spots with poles. Waste no time whatsoever. Probe thoroughly along the fall line with skis or with the heel ends of snowshoes. The most likely other place to search, after the above has failed, is in the main pile-up of snow at the bottom, or in any eddies where part of the slide stopped.

When an avalanche victim is located, his mouth and nose should be forcibly cleared of snow. Give mouth-to-mouth resuscitation. He should be examined for fractures and, if necessary, treated for shock. If a victim is not found, or for any reason it is necessary to ski a long distance for help, go at a moderate pace to avoid exhaustion because it may be necessary to lead a rescue party back to the site. At any rate, be able to describe the place exactly so that others can find it. And, of course, watch for other avalanche dangers en route.

Even as a busy, frequent skier and snowshoer, the odds are extremely high you will never encounter any avalanches. And knowing about them will certainly help you avoid them.

13

Where to Go: United States

JUST AS THERE ARE NO "MUSTS" concerning the clothing a ski-tourer wears, there are no absolutes in *where* to ski or snowshoe. If the snow at your home drifts to the level of the bedroom window sill, start there. Do you live near a golf course, a frozen stream, or on a snow-covered back road? Try that. Anywhere there is a reasonable expanse of snow cover can be your playground, and perhaps one of the nicest things about it is that you may easily have the area all to yourself and at no cost at all.

But let us assume you can't just roll out the front door onto a usable area. Or perhaps you're ready for new fields, have a weekend to spend, or are considering where to spend a mid-winter vacation. Where then? The choice is wide. Below you will find areas listed in 24 of our 50 states, and the list is probably far from complete. With the popularity of ski-touring growing so quickly, the facilities offered grow too, and an up-to-date listing is out-of-date almost before it leaves the presses.

Cross-country skiing, and often snowshoeing, routes are located in several different kinds of areas, and these differences largely determine the price range. For instance, ski-touring a route in a famous, expensive, distant Alpine ski resort will cost much more than following the power line right-of-way through a closer state park. Often the wealthy sportsman will prefer a wilderness trip and the middle-class skier save for a chic wallet-whipping tour. The destination you choose indicates only your preference, not your bank balance.

However, money, like calories, does count and to the tour operator particularly. To meet his growing costs in these inflationary days he must raise his prices at frequent intervals, as does everyone else. For this reason we are not quoting specific rates. Check yourself for the latest bad news.

To give a very general statement, count on spending $10 to $20 per day, often including some group lessons. An overnight will run much more, say, $20 to $30 including meals and lodging. Be sure to inquire whether you will be required to bring your own sleeping bag, and if you have none, whether one can be rented. Should you rent ski equipment, the charge, to now, has run very close to $6 per day. For touring, small groups are best, so further value can be squeezed from your dollar if you aren't one of a large gang. A half dozen people is a fine number, though many groups include up to twenty-five and some are even larger. Investigate what you are buying before counting out the money.

And now for the good news: Almost all places offer group rates, and many are extremely flexible in what their program will offer. They are able and willing to tailor a trip to your degree of expertise, your preferences in food, and the type of terrain you find most enjoyable. So don't be shy about creating your own group and inquiring about a custom tour at reasonable cost.

We have grouped the ski spots under five areas: Northeast, Mid-Atlantic, North Central, West, and Southwest. Alaska is saved for last and perhaps best, as it is in every sense a place apart.

THE NORTHEAST

Maine

Acadia National Park: This is definitely a place you should consider if finances are a determining factor in your selection—once you arrive, that is. Maine might just involve quite a commute. Being a national park, Acadia does not charge for the use of over 35 miles of beautiful scenic trails, all of which are well marked. Better still, for the very hardy type, there is a camping area about six miles from the beginning of the trails. If winter camping seems a bit too rugged, overnight accommodations are available five miles distant at Bar Harbor and Southwest Harbor. No lessons are available and there are no guided overnights. Begin your tour from the parking area off Route 198 in Northeast Harbor. Write: Superintendent, Acadia National Park, Route 1, Box 1, Bar Harbor, Maine 04609. Telephone: (207) 288-3338.

Akers Ski: Not far from the New Hampshire border, these Nordic ski-equipment people offer free ski-touring over 16 miles of well-marked and groomed trails. Equipment can be rented and there are lessons only if arranged in advance. Motel accommodations are over ten miles from Andover. Write: Leon Akers, Akers Ski, Andover, Maine 04216. Telephone: (207) 392-4582.

Bear Mountain Village: This is a full-service establishment in a remote wilderness area on South Pond in South Waterford. The Village has 50 miles of marked trails, and there is a charge only if the outing will include two meals during the day or will be an overnight stay. Equipment rental, instruction, and ski-packages of various lengths can be arranged. Write: Bear Mountain Village, Inc., RFD, Harrison, Maine 04040. Telephone: (207) 583-2541.

Evergreen Valley: Abutting White Mountain National Forest, this large 2000-acre complex offers everything—possibly more than you want. Ski-touring is only one of the many activities offered. Instruction at all levels is available from one of the 20 instructors; rentals available; rooms run from a single to dormitory accommodations. Dining ranges from the modest "Brown Bag" room through cafeteria to formal dining rooms. There are special ski packages. No fee is charged for the use of the trails, some of which are access routed to the national forest. Write: Evergreen Valley, East Stoneham, Maine 04231. Telephone: (207) 928-3300.

Pleasant Mountain: Alpine skiing is the main attraction here, so even the lower-cost packages include the cost of the lift ticket— and that's not pleasant. The six miles of trails in Bridgton are free to use, and equipment and lessons are available at the going rates. Overnight accommodations are available at the Pleasant Mountain Inn. The lodge offers any kind of dining you might prefer. Write: Pleasant Mountain Ski Area, Pleasant Mountain, Maine 04009. Telephone: (207) 647-2022.

Saddleback: The really serious skier—the kind who just won't go without knickers and who knows the technical terms for any maneuver—will love Saddleback. It offers a fully-accredited program where high school students can earn credit studying Alpine racing, freestyle or cross-country skiing. There are cross-country ski preparation lessons offered and even waxing classes. And for true chic, hear this: Low cost moonlight tours are run with wine, hamburgers, and hotdogs served. In addition, the 25 miles of trails are free, half- and full-day instruction is available, and rentals and lodging are right there at the mountain. Write: State of Maine Touring Center, Saddleback Mountain, Rangeley, Maine 04970. Telephone: (207) 864-3380.

Squaw Mountain: Greenville is just about in the center of the state of Maine and has 15 to 25 miles of marked, groomed trails. It is primarily for the beginning Nordic skier, but terrain for every level of expertise is available. Lodging, lessons, and gear for rent are all right at the mountain. Package tours for overnight, the weekend, or a week can be arranged. Write: Squaw Mountain, Greenville, Maine 04441. Telephone: (207) 695-2272.

Sugarloaf, U.S.A.: No one can complain about inflation when everything is free as it is here at sweet Sugarloaf. Both the seven-mile beginner trail and the nine-mile N.C.A.A. course are available as is a day-tour and (still free) moonlight trips complete with bonfire for warmth and atmosphere all under the protective eye of a guide. If you want to divest yourself of extra cash, you can do so by renting equipment, taking lessons and lodging, and treating yourself to the nightlife and food found right there at Sugarloaf. Write: Sugarloaf, U.S.A., Kingfield, Maine 04947. Telephone: (207) 237-2000.

Sunday River Ski Touring Center: This is a large place near Bethel which offers everything from free marked trails to free unmarked trails. B.Y.O. sleeping bag to the dorm or private room at the Sunday River Inn. You can rent equipment or not, take lessons or not, go on a package mid-week or weekend tour, or just arrive. There's lots of snow here from Thanksgiving to mid-April and not just on Sundays. Write: Sunday River Ski Touring Center, Sunday River Inn, Bethel, Maine 04217. Telephone: (207) 824-2410.

The Balsams Wilderness: After 94 years as a summer resort, this rambling (15,000-acre) tract opened during the winter eight years ago for skiing. It now has almost unlimited ski areas, both marked and maintained and unmarked. Lessons are available twice a day or for the whole day. Look into the package plans which include lessons, lodging, and meals. This, of course, is no tiny chalet, but a 450-bed hotel operating on Modified American Plan. Write: The Balsams, Dixfield Notch, New Hampshire 03576. Telephone: (603) 255-3400.

Bretton Woods: Stay at the famed old Mt. Washington Hotel or the Village Townhouse just off Route 302 during the week at a special rate, and ski the northern White Mountains. There is a small trail fee for the twice-weekly track-setter, and you may also avail yourself of the lessons and equipment at moderate cost. Consider the five-hour Bota Tour which includes equipment and lunch. They don't mention the contents of the bota but a brochure does claim: "We're in the Mt. Washington snow pocket. The snow falls earlier, falls heavier, falls longer. We've engineered our trails to hold every flake of precious snow." A recent inducement is the Geschmossel, a cross-country ski race which was reportedly a huge success. Write: The Sports Village at Bretton Woods, Bretton Woods, New Hampshire 03575. Telephone: (603) 278-5000.

Cannon Mountain: Old U.S. 3 and unused logging roads are now over five miles of ski trails in Franconia Notch State Park. This Cannon Mountain area is probably the oldest cross-country ski area in America, as it was in this vicinity that the Nansen Ski Club of Berlin, New Hampshire, skied over a century ago. Instruction and equipment rentals are available at Peabody Slopes Building. The primary beginning spot is a parking lot at Echo Lake, but there is a secondary spot at the northern end near Exit 36 on Interstate 93. Write: Cannon Mountain, Franconia, New Hampshire 03580. Telephone: (603) 823-5563.

Emerson Hill Touring Center: As you enter Fitchburg, Massachusetts, to find lodging (none is closer) and discover it to be snowless, despair not. Emerson may well be under a comfortable blanket of white. These 15 miles of maintained trails in the Wapack

Range weave back and forth over the state line at 1500 feet above sea level. The Touring Center is three miles northwest of Ashby, Massachusetts. Look for A & D Nordic Sports signs in New Ipswich, New Hampshire, near the Mt. Watatic parking lot. Should you purchase a cross-country ski outfit here, you are entitled to a free two-hour lesson. On a regular basis there are lessons in small groups, and the usual rentals are available. Write: Emerson Hill Ski Touring Center, Page Hill Road, New Ipswich, New Hampshire 03071. Telephone: (603) 878-1863.

EMS Touring Center: Eastern Mountain Sports of Boston is the Sears & Roebuck of the outdoor equipment retail and mail-order business. In conjunction with the branch in North Conway is the Sports Ski Touring Center at the old Intervale ski area. Over 200 sets of rental equipment are available—with wax—and certified teachers give both private and group instruction. This is a large operation with much evening entertainment, facilities, and lodging choices in either Intervale or North Conway. They also throw informal ski races mid-weekly, and on alternate weekends with Jackson (see below) they host larger events. Write: EMS Ski Touring Center, Intervale, New Hampshire 03845. Telephone: (603) 356-5606.

Gray Ledges: Set on 1300 acres with five miles of trails (perhaps more by now) Gray Ledges is an Interdenominational Christian Conference Center with a lodge and old barns converted to dormitories. There are no rentals, but lessons are available. A small daily fee is charged with a moderate overnight charge which includes dinner and breakfast. Bring your own sleeping bag, and pay less. Get there by taking Interstate 89, then go west from Exit 13, turn right before the bridge, and go up the hill one mile to the group of red buildings. Write: Gray Ledges, Grantham, New Hampshire 03753. Telephone: (603) 863-9880.

Gunstock: A smaller, simpler place, Gunstock in Gilford offers the free use of five miles of trails, marked and maintained. Rentals are optional as are instructions. Closest lodging is a mile away at The Arlberg. Write Gunstock Ski Area, Box 336, Laconia, New Hampshire 03246. Telephone: (603) 293-4342.

Jackson Ski Touring Center: This is like no other place you've seen. The small village of Jackson envisioned and then set about to complete 75 miles of trails through White Mountain National Forest, and on adjacent private properties which connect every

All across the United States, facilities for ski-tourers are being created around the major downhill ski resorts.

inn, lodge, and hotel in the area. Without stopping, the skier can visit the picturesque town, the forest, and Alpine facilities at Black, Tyrol, and Wildcat. The Touring Center Office hands out a trail map and gives information on current snow conditions. You pay a $1 fee if you're not a member of the Jackson Ski Touring Club. There are first-aid stations and emergency telephones. All types of instruction are available as are packages offering every combination you could think of. Tours? Of course. Everything. Lodging runs from bunkrooms to hotels and après-ski life is described as "active." You can also participate in other winter activities at this complex. Transportation is easy from anywhere. Write: Jackson Ski Touring Foundation, Jackson, New Hampshire 03846. Telephone: (603) 383-4326.

Loon Mountain: Start here and it is possible to ski on 100 miles of trail and never ride on your own tracks. Loon Mountain itself has nine miles of trail that are maintained by grooming machines, but these, mostly in the White Mountain preserve, connect with the White Mountain National Forest network. Within this vast range it is possible to encounter every conceivable type of country from mountain peak to flat scrub woods. Some skilled individuals follow the ridge trail 15 miles to Galehead Hut where it meets the Appalachian Trail. Instruction is available, and equipment rental rates drop significantly with long-term agreements. There are day, overnight, and moonlight tours. Lodging available within 15 miles. Write: Loon Mountain, Lincoln, New Hampshire 03251. Telephone: (603) 745-8111.

Pole and Pedal Shop: This one is open all year, but caters to cross-country skiers during the winter. It keeps 15 miles of trails machine-groomed from voluntary donations. Group lessons and rentals are available singly or as a package. P & P has a program for school racing and occasionally stages time trials and informal races. The shop is located at the intersection of Routes 202 and 114, three miles from Exit 5 on Interstate 89. Write: Pole and Pedal Shop, Route 114, Henniket, New Hampshire 03242. Telephone: (603) 428-3292.

Temple Mountain: Just four miles east of Peterborough and 63 miles from Boston, this area offers everything for the skier in the way of equipment, instruction, and tours on their 35 miles of marked trails. There is a trail fee. Gear can be purchased (a good waxing service is part of it) or rented for either a half or full day. A hundred sets of rental equipment are on hand, so perfect fit is ensured. Half- or full-day lessons are available, and there are long tours up Mt. Monadnock or short ones with wine and cheese. (How about two short ones?) A package price for rental, lesson, and lunch is possible. Clinics on technique, care of equipment, and waxing are held, as are outings for intermediate and advanced skiers to remote lakes and ponds. These are prescheduled, so be sure to inquire ahead for dates and new information. Write: Temple Mountain Ski Area, Route 101, Peterborough, New Hampshire 03458. Telephone: (603) 924-6469.

Waterville Valley has all the usual features and some very original and unique ones as well. For the usual, there are 11 miles of well-kept and patrolled trails plus 35 more miles of terrain presenting new challenges for the more advanced skier. There is a nominal trail fee here (more on weekends); lessons are given and various packages for mid-week or weekend skiing are available. The unique feature of Waterville Valley is the stress put on environmental considerations. There is a self-guiding nature trail, talks are given to groups, and informal discussions with the personnel over a hot cup of coffee. Facts and their interrelationships are more visible out of doors, and most clients come away feeling more aware of their surroundings than they were before their arrival. Write: Waterville Valley Ski Touring Center, Waterville Valley, New Hampshire 03223. Telephone: (603) 236-8311.

Whitaker Woods: Some years ago there was a bequest of 150 acres of land for public enjoyment with the proviso that no mechanized vehicles could violate the peace to be found here. So, it's yours. Enjoy it. The tract is located just behind the Pine School in North Conway, and while the trails are mostly unmarked, they are easy to find with the map available at the EMS shop. Write: Eastern Mountain Sports, Main Street, North Conway, New Hampshire 03860. Telephone: (603) 356-5433.

Windblown in this case doesn't mean your hat is torn off from the gust of a near-collision with another skier. In this area just north of the Massachusetts state line the skier who yearns for quiet and isolation can use fourteen miles of trails in relative solitude, since once the tiny parking lot is filled, no one else is admitted. There are small trail fees (youngsters free), and there is even a hut far in the woods warmed by a wood stove. Rentals and lessons are available. Reach this place of peace by first going to Fitchburg, then north to New Ipswich and following the signs. Write: Windblown, RFD, New Ipswich, New Hampshire 03071. Telephone: (603) 878-2861.

Wolfeboro is not a ski area in the usual sense. Wolfeboro, in fact, is a town, and the skiing available here is appealing for a different sort of outing. The touring is through a local club, the Abenaki Outing Club, and trails run through woods, beside lakes and homes, and along old logging roads, all on private property. There is no charge, but donations to the club for trail maintenance are appreciated. The tourist facilities of the town are numerous including box lunches. Packages can be arranged, as can gear rental and lessons. The trails are not patrolled, so you are urged to sign in and out. Write: Nordic Ski Shop, Box 297, Clow Road, Wolfeboro, N.H. 03894. Telephone: (603) 569-3724.

Vermont

Blueberry Hill Touring Center is the warm and glowing heart of the Vermont Ski Touring Club located in the wilds of the Green Mountain National Forest. The Blueberry Inn, once a blacksmith shop, is also a warming-waxing room for skiers and can accommodate 16 overnight guests and provide them with meals. A potbelly stove is always banked to warm coals and holds a pot of steaming soup (gratis). The 22 miles of trails were cut especially for cross-country skiing by club members and are maintained by them. They are free to Inn guests and club members; otherwise there is a small charge. Instruction, gear rental, and box lunches are a bit pricey, but may be worth it. There are no packages. The skiing here, as you might expect, is on the challenging side. There are two overnight stops. A whole day's skiing brings you to Middlebury College Snow Bowl. Be alert to find Blueberry Hill—it's off Route 73 in Goshen. Ask for more detailed directions when you contact Blueberry Hill Ski Touring Center, Goshen, Vt. 05733. Telephone: (802) 267-6735.

Bolton Valley should be headquarters for the experienced skier with a flattened wallet. Here, between Burlington and Montpelier, he can find 20 miles of trails which are part of the Long Trail System including a 17-mile expert trail to Stowe. No fee is charged for these well-groomed paths. Package prices are available for five- and seven-day private lessons or group instruction. Gear can be rented at the going rate, and lodging is at the resort and nearby motels. Write: Bolton Valley Corporation, Bolton, Vermont 05477.

Burke Mountain is as full of packages as Santa's pack. There are special midweek and week arrangements; a three-day lesson plan, a 5½-day plan, and a full week. Colored discs and arrows define the 32 miles of groomed trails, and you'll pay a small fee for their use. Guided tours, half-day group lessons which "stress personal attention" and gear rental are all available. There is "Town House" living where a maximum of ten persons share four bedrooms, four baths, dishwasher, and fireplace on a daily or weekly basis. Then there's the "Wall House," a similar arrangement but accommodating only six at a very reasonable per person daily rate. For a concentrated skiing experience look into the Burke all-day clinic. Write: Burke Mountain Recreation Inc., East Burke, Vermont 05832. Telephone: (802) 626-3305.

Dakin's Vermont Mountain Shop feels that anyone can learn ski-touring in a relatively short time, and proves it on woodsy trails. You may have private, semi-private, or group instruction. Rentals with lessons are available as a package. There's a small building warmed by a wood stove for recuperation and waxing, with free soup or tea provided. Write: Dakin's, Ferrisburg, Vermont 05456. Telephone: (802) 877-2936.

Darion Inn Touring Center boasts over 70 miles of trails, only some of which are well maintained. There is a small daily fee charged, and for this you may tour logging trails along the river or take the sugaring tour over fields with a view of Burke Mountain, Willoughby Gap, and the beautiful Vermont landscape. Rentals and both private and group instruction are available. Farm buildings have been converted, and private, semi-private, and dorm accommodations are available—with or without meals. Write: Ski Touring Center, Darion Inn, East Burke, Vermont 05832.

Edison Hill Manor is a country inn on 400 acres of woodland with miles of marked trails, good food, spring water, and serene vistas to enjoy. Full- and half-day rentals are available as is a midweek package which includes instruction, rentals, two meals, lodging, and use of trails. All this at 1500 feet at Route 1, Stowe, Vermont 05672. Telephone: (802) 253-7371.

Equinox Touring Center has five miles of groomed trails and three times that length of unmaintained trails around Mt. Equinox in Manchester, Vermont. Group or private lessons are available at slightly higher than the usual rates, but the rental costs are less than average. There is a nice package for two persons which includes a double room, breakfast, and cross-country clinic with use of the trails. Group discounts are given. Lodging is available at the center, and there is a new restaurant which serves country dishes. Write: Equinox Touring Center, Manchester, Vermont 05254.

Farm Motor Inn & Country Club might be just right for the newcomer who is not frantic for wilderness and silence. The facilities are small, and no one will be lost track of, although there are 280 acres of farm land to explore. Equipment rentals are very low and day tours are offered. Write: RFD Box 180, Morrisville, Vermont 05661. Telephone: (802) 888-4913.

Glen Ellyn claims its ten miles of marked trails are groomed daily. At this well-known Alpine resort you may avail yourself of half-day lessons with full- or half-day rentals at a moderate price. Write: Glen Ellyn Ski Area, RFD Box 66, Waitsfield, Vermont 05673.

Green Trails is one place where you can ski and snowshoe, too. There are also sleighrides, tobogganning, and sledding on 25 miles of marked trails. A network of routes for beginners lies in Allis State Park, and both learners and intermediates may tour an eight-mile trail through evergreen woods and sugar maples. Facilities are free to Inn guests, but they'd like a small sum for trail maps. Instruction and rentals are possible, also discounts for stays of over five nights. Single and double rooms are available at rather high rates, and there is a lounge which serves lunches and toe-warming drinks. If you'll be on the trail at midday, arrange for a picnic lunch if you like. Green Trails is south of Montpelier off Route 89 near Randolph Center. There should be snow here by November, and to avoid slippery roads, choose Amtrack—it goes right to Montpelier. Write: Green Trails Inn & Ski Touring Center, By the Floating Bridge, Brookfield, Vermont 05036. Telephone: (802) 276-2012.

Hermitage Inn is more accessible than other places, situated as it is in southern Vermont on 100 acres. There is no charge for use of the facilities, and trails are marked and groomed with both snowmobiles and trackers. Two-hour instruction is available, and there are several ski packages. Write: The Hermitage, Box 291, Coldbrook Road, Wilmington, Vermont 05363.

Highland Lodge Touring isn't too far from Montpelier/Barre. In fact, if you get that far yourself, the Lodge will take you the rest of the way. More than fifteen miles of trails glide past lovely views of fields and woods and past Caspian Lake. There is no charge, and no trails are groomed except those especially for the novice. Half- and full-day instruction are available as is an expensive one-hour private lesson. Rentals run less than average. The lodge offers many accommodation options: single; two or three persons; a cottage for four (but can cram six); and a housekeeping unit. Write: Highland Lodge, Greensboro, Vermont 05841.

The late afternoon sun sets outside a snowshoe camp and creates a magically beautiful time of any trip.

Killington Ski Area is a large, well-known Alpine area with great varieties of lodging available, some within a mile of the ski area, some much farther. Located in central Vermont, it offers 5 ½ miles of trails that wind up and slide down through and past all sorts of terrain. There are many instructional options: full and half days, with and without gear, lower prices for children, and an all-day tour with backpack lunch included. For much more information write Killington Lodging Bureau, 302 Killington Road, Killington, Vermont 05751 or Killington Ski Resort, Cross-Country, Killington, Vermont 05751.

Mountain Top Inn: Plastic, brightly colored flags mark the 45 miles of maintained trails which lead over hills, past the reservoir, and through the woods. The trails, on 600 acres, are maintained for a small donation from users. Rentals and half- and full-day instruction are available. Ski packages are offered, and the rates at the Inn are moderate with small reductions for children. Go on a tour of your own or one that's guided. Either way, keep an eye out for the porcupine. His name is Jonathan. The Inn is eight miles northeast of Rutland. Write: Mountain Top Inn, Chittenden, Vermont 05737.

Mt. Snow offers cross-country skiing as just one of its attractions. It is the largest ski area in southern Vermont and has 12 to 15 miles of maintained trails. Instruction and rentals are available as are moonlight tours. For a list of the numerous near-by and trail-side lodging possibilities write Ski School, Mt. Snow Development Corp., Mt. Snow, Vermont 05356.

Okemo has 14 miles of trails, largely unmaintained. Only small numbers of visitors are accommodated at one time, and the terrain cruises gently through woods and evergreen clumps, crosses meadows and alder swamps, and parallels small streams and dams. Instruction and rental gear run far lower than you might expect, and any rental fees are credited to the purchase of equipment. There are several low-priced motels and inns from which to choose. Write: Snowtown Inns, P.O. Box 62, Ludlow, Vermont 05149 or Ski School Director, Okemo Mts., RFD 1, Ludlow, Vermont 05149.

Smuggler's Notch is an entire area which can sleep one thousand tired bodies at the same time in its $10-million recreation community. Drive to northern Vermont via Routes 89, 15, and finally 108, or take the bus to Burlington where a complimentary Notch bus will pick you up. Instruction is available, as are rentals and guided tours. You may also go alone on the 25 miles of trails with a surprising variety of terrain. All trails are coded as to difficulty. Moonlight tours are popular and wind up with wine and cheese parties. There's a waxing clinic, too. Write: Director of Skiing Services, Smuggler's Notch Ski Area, Jeffersonville, Vermont 05464.

Sonnenhof Inn is a family place offering free use of logging roads for trails. No rentals. Tourers are often accompanied by a child or dog (or both) of the proprietors, who run a country inn with good food and even a heated pool. Write: Sonnenhof Inn, Route 242, Jay, Vermont 05859.

Stratton Mountain Ski Area has 11 miles of trails which either circle the golf course or wind up to the top of Stratton Mountain. The more difficult terrain is also more interesting, passing ponds, woodland, and historical monuments en route. Group lessons and tours are offered as are rather costly rentals. There are many hotels close by this southern Vermont area which is off Route 100 and about 15 miles from Manchester. Write: Stratton Mountain Ski Area, Stratton Mountain, Vermont 05155. (802) 297-2200.

Sugarbush Inn Cross-Country & Ski-Touring Center is in northern Vermont just off that familiar Route 100. There are 40 miles of varied trails, most marked. You may glide past creeks, over a golf course, and through the woods. Four miles from Sugarbush is Glen Ellyn, and the confident skier can just ski across a ridge to reach it. There are private and group lessons and full- and half-day rentals, all just a bit on the expensive side. Picnic tours are fun, and moonlight skis are popular, too. "If the moon isn't out, we use headlights." The Inn is just at the access point to the ski area. Write: Sugarbush Inn, Warren, Vt. 05674. Telephone: (802) 583-2341.

Trapp Family Lodge, owned by the Sound of Music family, sits on 1000 acres of glorious Vermont countryside and is woven together by 50 miles of groomed and marked trails. A cabin in the woods serves lunch, or you can eat picnic style. This is the place to go if you really want to learn to ski. The cadre includes former Olympic skiers who teach groups and give private lessons for no more than you would pay elsewhere. Rental prices are lower than usual, but add a small additional fee for the use of the trails if you are not staying at the lodge. Look into the Learn to Ski packages offered. Write: Trapp Family Lodge, Stowe, Vermont 05672.

Viking Touring Center offers inexpensive rentals and instruction. If you want something in addition, check into X-C workshops, ski-week packages, waxing clinics, and overnights. Twenty-five miles of trails, marked and patrolled, cross over open fields, woodlands, old logging roads, and puddles and ponds. To venture out on your own, just go on into the Green Mountain National Forest. There is a heated hut for waxing or thawing the body. The trails are free and there's always plenty of hot coffee or tea at the Center. Lodging is at nearby Post Horn and the Dostals. Write: Viking Ski Touring Center, Little Pond Road, Londonderry, Vermont 05148. Telephone: (802) 824-3933.

Woodstock Touring Center has no concerts, but the country club, about a half mile from the Inn, offers 35 miles of trails for every level of competence. There are touring clinics, races, and even a nature tour with a forester. Rentals are available, and there are cabins with fireplaces to warm you. A small trail fee is charged. There are week and weekend ski packages, too. Stay at the Woodstock Inn or a local motel. Write: Woodstock Inn Ski Touring Center, Woodstock, Vermont 05091.

Massachusetts

Broadmoor/Little Pond is a wildlife sanctuary and therefore rather small and vulnerable to attack from large and/or boisterous groups. For the skier who enjoys his surroundings more than his sport, this is a favorite place, with only 6½ miles of nature trails. No rentals, no après-ski anything. Drive one mile south of South Natick on Route 16 (Eliot Street) to South Street. Bear left on South and proceed ½ mile to the parking lot. Don't slam the door. Write: Broadmoor/Little Pond Sanctuary, Natick, Massachusetts 01760.

Holyoke: Located in the Connecticut River Valley, the Wycoff Park Country Club has opened its golf course to winter use by ski-tourers. There is a large selection of equipment for sale or rent.

Jug End Resort is a small, informal area two miles southwest of the junction of Routes 23 and 41. Instruction is available, and there is a snack bar. Box lunches can be provided, too, for enjoyment on one of the two eight-mile trails. Write: Jug End Resort, South Egremont, Massachusetts 01258. Telephone: (413) 528-0434.

Putterham Meadows Golf Course can arrange for rentals and offers 12 miles of trails, all marked with flags. There is a ski-trail leader, and this is the closest area for Bostonians to ski-tour. Write: Putterham Meadows Golf Course, 1281 West Roxbury Parkway, Brookline, Massachusetts 02167. Telephone: (617) 566-5008.

Waubeeka Touring Center is a golf course during the summer, and its 150 acres of gently rolling terrain are excellent for the novice who can avail himself of the services of qualified instructors either with a group or solo. There is a ski shop, or you may rent the equipment. The clubhouse is a country club, not the shack/hut shelter associated with ski-touring. The trails are maintained with donations from users. Accomplished skiers may cruise off into the adjacent Brodie Mountains to conquer ten miles of trails, or go off to the east to Mount Greylock Reservation, either on a guided tour or alone. In keeping with the almost posh atmosphere here, there are excellent restaurants with motels to match within quick driving distance. Write: Waubeeka Ski Touring Center, Williamstown, Massachusetts 02167. Telephone: (413) 458-3000.

Connecticut

Blackberry River Inn Touring Center doesn't mean only ski-touring. You may also snowshoe, toboggan ride, sled, or ice skate. Forsaking all these, you may just eschew exertion altogether and laze about in the "Ice House." Lessons are available on the 20 miles of marked, groomed trails for half or full days (with lunch). Equipment may be rented, and there is a small trail fee. A five-day all-inclusive package is available, and it includes a goatskin of wine and a snack for the trail. It is on Route 44 north of New Haven. Write: Blackberry River Inn Ski Touring Center, Route 44, Norfolk, Connecticut 06058. Telephone: (203) 542-5100.

Powder Ridge has only five miles of its own trails, but these are adjacent to 30 more miles of state hiking trails which, when snow-covered, are used by skiers. Guided tours and instruction are available, and there is a reasonably priced package for beginners. Shops in the area carry a line of equipment and offer a fall clinic. Exit 17 on Route 91. Write: Powder Ridge Ski Area, Middlefield, Connecticut 06455.

THE MIDDLE ATLANTIC STATES

New York

Adirondack Loj: The state of New York provides 12 miles of ski trails at the Mt. Van Hoevenberg Recreation Area, and just next door is the Loj, operated by the Adirondack Mountain Club. The two areas are connected and can be used as one. This large network of trails is south of Lake Placid, at Heart Lake. Lodging at the Loj can mean staying in a bunkhouse or private room. There is a dining room, and gear can be rented or purchased. If you want lessons, ask. Write: Adirondack Loj, Box 967, Lake Placid, New York 12946. Telephone: (518) 523-3441.

Apple Barn is frequented largely by local skiers who come to enjoy not only the apple pie, but the 180 acres of orchard land. There are five miles of maintained (with a snowmobile tracksled), marked trails available free of charge. There is a shop here with rental gear at very reasonable rates, and half-day lessons are given. You will also find a restaurant and country store, but the nearest lodging is in Schenectady. Write: Hanson's Trail North, 960-A, Troy-Schenectady Rd., Latham, New York 12110. Telephone: (518) 399-6111.

Belleayre Mountain has several short tracks running from its base, but cross-country skiers usually prefer the ridge route which runs along the top of the lifts and leads to neighboring Highmount Ski Area. Both Alpine and cross-country skiing are offered here in the Catskills, 35 miles west of Kingston on Route 28. If you don't have your own gear, stop en route at the Scandinavian Ski Shop and rent it there. Instruction is available both for full- and half-days, and the activity stops at dark. Write: Belleayre Mountain Ski Center, Pine Hill, New York 12465. Telephone: (914) 254-5601.

Country Hills Farm consists of evergreen woods, a stand of maple trees complete with sugar shed, and open land, all overlaid with 12 miles of maintained trails available for a modest fee. Equipment rents for a very small sum although instruction is more expensive than usual. The farm is immediately south of Syracuse on Interstate 81. Take Exit 14 and turn left at the center of Tully for about two miles. Write: Country Hills Farm, North Road, Tully, New York. Telephone: (315) 696-8774.

Garnet Hill Lodges consist of Big Shanty and The Log House, both of which have double rooms with private bath and two meals at a very reasonable rate. Housekeeping accommodations are available, and there's a nice midweek package. For novice and intermediate skiers there are ten miles of maintained trails free to lodge guests or, for a nominal fee, for visitors. More experienced skiers may wish to venture out into the surrounding wilderness at Gore Mountain. Rentals and instructional packages are available at Duffany's Ski Shop. Possibly best of all, Garnet Hill is only about a four-hour drive from New York City, northwest of Warrensburg

Guided winter hikes on snowshoes are free in many state and national parks.

on Thirteenth Lake. Write: Garnet Hill Lodges, North River, New York 02856. Telephone: (518) 998-2821.

Innsbruck USA has an instruction area made especially for the novice, and it offers half-day lessons and reasonable rentals. Everything is a bit higher on weekends. Twenty miles of trails are available. Nearest lodging is at Binghamton, four miles distant and very close to the Pennsylvania border. Write: Innsbruck USA, Box 598, Binghamton, New York 13909. Telephone: (607) 669-4191.

Lake Minnewaska: Cross-country skiing has come to the Catskills! Accommodations run the full gamut from "running water" to private bath, none of it inexpensive. Instruction is not cheap, and trail fees are steep, too. But food and people and après-ski life it has—and so much closer than Vermont or New Hampshire. There are buses and trains from New York City and even a door-to-door limousine service from the metropolitan area. Write: Lake Minnewaska Resort, Lake Minnewaska, New York 12561. Telephone: (914) 255-6000.

Lake Mohonk is just five miles west of New Paltz and easy and quick to reach from New York City via the Thruway. The 7500 acres of land have been in the same family since just after the Civil War. The guest skier stays at Mohonk House, a vast old building with roaring fires and an air of past nobility-gentility. Outside are 90 miles of trails threading their way over and around a golf course and a virgin stand of hemlocks. Lake Mohonk is not in a heavy-snow belt, but not much is necessary to make the graveled avenues (made for horse-drawn carriages) acceptable. Other, steeper paths require more cover and may or may not have it. A huge midday meal is served at a reasonable cost, and the price of daily trail fees is deducted. Yearly rates are attractive if you can come up often. The American Plan room rates are average or a bit above, while gear-rental costs are low. If there's a new heavy snow cover though, get there early, for the supply won't last long. Write: Lake Mohonk, New Paltz, New York 12561. Telephone: (914) 255-1000.

Mt. Van Hoevenberg is the place for you if you have no need for instruction, rentals, or fondu. It is run free of charge by the state of New York and has 12 miles of carefully maintained trails in a set of ten loops which originate at the parking lot. They are all color-coded, and something for every level of competence can be found. Closest lodging is at Lake Placid, five miles distant. Write: New York State Department of Environmental Conservation, 50 Wolf Road, Albany, New York 12202. Telephone: (518) 457-2500.

Old Forge and the neighboring town of Inlet have between them 32 miles of ski trails, all marked and maintained. There is no charge for their use, and anything you need to know, rent, or learn can be arranged at The Ski Touring Center in Old Forge at the junction of Route 28 and South Shore Road. The area is a summer resort now opened in the winter too, with a large complement of accommodations and eating facilities. It is at the eastern end of the Fulton Chain Lakes. For more explicit directions, write: Central Adirondack Association, Old Forge, New York 13420. Telephone: (315) 369-6983.

Paleface Ski Center has a lodge where you may stay; it rents boots and poles and even offers informal instruction. (Formal lessons are given, but that's 15 miles away.) There are 25 miles of marked, maintained trails free to all here near Lake Placid. Write:

Paleface Ski Center, Route 86, Box 163, Jay, New York 12941. Telephone: (518) 946-2272.

Palisades Interstate Park Commission maintains six ski trails of over 31 miles in the beautiful Bear Mountain area. Of course they're free to all, although there's a small charge for maps. There are three factors you should know: No rentals are available; no instruction is given; and often there is no snow—so check first. On the other hand, the area is a nice drive north from the George Washington Bridge on the Palisades Parkway. Write: Supervisor of Camps and Recreational Activities, Palisades Interstate Park Commission, Bear Mountain, New York 10911. Telephone: (914) 786-2701.

Scotch Valley has rental equipment and full- and half-day lessons. There are 15 miles of trails, only three of which are groomed; all are marked, however. Lodging is available at Stamford. Exit from the Thruway at the Catskill turn-off and take Route 23 westbound for about 40 miles. Write: Scotch Valley Ski School, Stamford, New York 12167. Telephone: (607) 652-7332.

Williams Lake Hotel has a full equipment line for rent (reasonable) plus very reasonable instruction plus a "registration charge" rather higher than usual. There are marked trails, about 15 miles of them, half groomed and half *au naturel*. This is the New Paltz area again, seven miles north on Route 32 in Rosendale. Write: Williams Lake Hotel, Rosendale, New York 14272. Telephone: (914) 658-6141.

New Jersey

McAfee is mainly a downhill ski area, but if you will spend a moderate amount for the lift, you may ski ten miles of trails through the Hamburg Mountain Game Preserve. Two miles are especially for beginners, three for the expert. Check snow cover before you go. Write: Great Gorge Ski Area, McAfee, New Jersey 07428. Telephone: (201) 827-9146.

Sleepy Hollow Park, situated as it is in New Jersey, has a minimal snow cover, but after a good fall you might like to tour the trails which spread over 300 acres of gently sloping terrain. There are special trails for beginners, mediums, and experts, and the area is three miles from the Playboy Club Hotel, if that helps your orientation. Write: Area Manager, RD #2, Box 145A, Sussex, New Jersey 07601. Telephone: (201) 875-6211.

Pennsylvania

Black Forest Ski Touring has two things going for it: One, there are over 22 miles of track and two, it's free. It's all part of the Tiadaghton State Forest in Williamsport. On the other side, the trails are all that's offered. There is no lodging, tours, rentals, or instruction, and the closest place to spend the night is Waterville. This just might cut down on the number of people who come here, so if solitude is desirable, try it. Write: Pennsylvania Department of Environmental Resources, District Forester, Bureau of Forestry, 423 East Central Avenue, South Williamsport, Pennsylvania 17701. Telephone: (717) 326-3576.

French Creek State Park is fortunate enough to have a relatively high elevation, which means that although it is situated in the southeastern part of the state it still has enough snow to support ski-touring on its 6000 acres. One trail called Buzzard climbs to 1000 feet, dips, and then rises again to 1600 feet for a fine view of the area. The trails are marked and will suit either the beginner or the more experienced skier. Off-trail skiing is also possible. Write: French Creek State Park, RD #1, Elverson, Pennsylvania 19520. Telephone: (215) 582-8125.

Virginia

Mt. Rogers National Recreation Area has a high elevation and offers 20 miles of trails over its 5000 acres south of Interstate 81. Write: Appalachian Outfitters, 215 North Main Street, Blacksburg, Virginia 24060. Telephone: (703) 951-2600.

West Virginia

Monongahela National Forest: The skier uses a network of un-plowed logging roads and climbs to Spruce Knob, West Virginia's highest point (4863 feet) in this, the Cranberry Back Country. Write: Forest Service Office, Richwood, West Virginia 26261. Telephone: (304) 846-6558.

Snowshoe offers inexpensive instruction, guided tours, and rentals at the going daily rate, which decreases over the rental period. The heart of the area is the summit, reached by lift, for which there is a fee. Once on top, there are lounges offering refreshment (but no lodging) and the beginning of the trails which wind down over routes of varying difficulty to the foot. Find the place 40 miles south of Elkins on Route 219. Write: Snowshoe, Slaty Fork, West Virginia 26291. Telephone: (304) 799-6600.

THE NORTH CENTRAL STATES

Michigan

Birchwood Farm Lodge exists mainly for the summer visitor and has accommodations for 150 people, but during the winter the cross-country skier is king; no snowmobiles are allowed, and although there is plenty of downhill activity nearby, Birchwood is strictly Nordic. On its 1000 acres of land are three trails: one, three, or five milers. Lake Michigan is right there and is occasionally viewed from the scenic trails. Sleigh rides and night touring, complete with wine and fondu, can be arranged, and rentals and tour guides are available from Bahnhof Ski Shop in Petoskey. Birchwood has an average-priced ski package and is located on Highway 131. Write: Birchwood Farm Lodge, Harbor Springs, Michigan 49740. Telephone: (616) 526-2151.

Pine Mountain Ski Area is mainly an Alpine skiing resort with heated pool and (sadly) snowmobile tours, but it also offers ski-touring and snow camping. It is surrounded by state forests which add great new dimensions to the stay. There are ski packages which include lodging, meals, and lessons, with nice discounts for children. Write: Pine Mountain Corp., Pine Mountain Road, Star Route 2, Iron Mountain, Michigan 49801. Telephone: (906) 774-2747.

Ranch Rudolf has it all. For beginners there are two-, six-, and nine-mile trail loops, all groomed (as all trails are) by the only

machine allowed on the grounds. There is a 13-mile track for the
expert, and the ranch's tree-studded acreage, garnished with lakes
and streams, abuts 123,000 acres of Fife Lake State Forest for more
snowy expanse than you could ever use. Use of the trails is free
to the public, and the lodge's log buildings accommodate 78. Rentals are inexpensive, but ski packages are higher than other places.
It may be worth it though—they offer ski-joring, using huskies
instead of horses to tow the skier. The gung-ho skier can even
backpack to several prepared campsites to spend the night. With
any luck the oil explorers presently on the prowl won't find any
and the planned new ski trail can commence. The ranch is 12
miles southeast of Traverse City in the Boardman River Valley.
Write: Ranch Rudolf, P.O. Box 587, Traverse City, Michigan
49684.

Schuss Mountain offers both cross-country skiing and snowshoeing, and you can rent gear for either. It is also a downhill
area, and the purchase of a lift ticket is mandatory. However, the
winter sportsman staying on a ski package may exchange the ticket
for a pass and a Lover's Lunch of bread, cheese, fruit, and beverage,
which seems fair enough. Ski or snowshoe on 20 miles of marked
trails. Instruction is available. Write: Schuss Mountain, Mancelona,
Michigan 49659. Telephone: (616) 587-9162.

Shanty Creek Lodge is in Bellaire, very near Schuss Mountain,
and has 15 miles of marked trails. There is no charge here, but
full-day rentals and half-day instruction are available. Write:
Shanty Creek Lodge, Bellaire, Michigan 49615. Telephone: (616)
533-8621.

Sugar Loaf Village has 13 miles of maintained trails which are
divided according to their difficulty. The trail fee is comparatively
stiff as is the price of a brief lesson. Average-priced rentals are
available with discounts for groups. There are occasional moonlight tours. Write: Sugar Loaf Village, RR #1, Cedar, Michigan
49621. Telephone: (616) 228-5461.

Suicide Bowl isn't a name designed to pull in the quiet ski-tourer
who desires tranquility and the pursuit of his own pace. This area
on the Upper Peninsula does draw jumpers who perform on the
70-meter hill. (Even the use of the metric system smacks of continental competition.) The ski-tour trails are there, however, and
for the skier who wants to push himself a bit along ridges, up

through wooded paths, and down fairly difficult slopes, this is the place. The use of the trails is free, and there are no rentals. The bowl isn't far from the National Hall of Fame at Ishpeming where there is also lodging. For touring information, write: The Bietila Sport Shop, 107 Division Street, Ishpeming, Michigan 49849. For lodging information write: Ishpeming Chamber of Commerce, 202 East Division Street, Ishpeming, Michigan 49849.

Minnesota

Hennepin County Park, just 20 miles from Minneapolis, offers 30 miles of marked trails for the use of the public. There is a small daily parking fee, or a very moderate annual ticket can be purchased. Rentals are available at the nearby Baker Hyland Lake Park Reserve. Write: Hennepin County Park Reserve District, Route 1, Maple Plain, Minnesota 55359.

Lutsen is one of those lucky places located next to a national forest, in this case Superior National Forest. Ten miles of trails are maintained, but there is a huge network which exists unmarked and unpatrolled. Lutsen has lessons, rentals, and many different package plans. Every plan allows children up to ten to come along free. Write: Lutsen Resort, Lutsen, Minnesota 55612. Telephone: (218) 663-7212.

Quadna Mountain itself is a 325-foot rounded glacial formation with a chalet at its foot. The ski-tourer can explore here on the lodge's 1200 acres and also on the neighboring state forest land. One mile away is the four-season lodge, a rustic 48-room structure beside what is a golf course during the summer and trails when snow covered. Be warned that snowmobiles are also welcomed here. The lodge is classy, with two cocktail lounges, a sauna, and a rec room. It is 150 miles north of the Twin Cities. Write: Quadna Mountain, Hill City, Minnesota 55748. Telephone: (218) 697-2324.

Sugar Hills Ski Area has everything for pre, during, and après-ski, including a country store, an inn, and a sauna. There are also 35 miles of free and unmaintained trails, all marked. They cross brooks and run beside a lake. There are even picnic sites. Rentals are possible, as is instruction. Inquire about the worthwhile ski

Several areas offer special reduced rates for children, and in a few places kids are admitted free.

package. Write: Sugar Hills Ski Area, Box 369, Grand Rapids, Minnesota 55744. Telephone: (218) 326-3473.

Wisconsin

Blackhawk Ridge has 40 miles of trails over 600 private acres of land at the border of the Mazomanie Wildlife Area. The area is closed to snowmobiles and accommodates up to 40 families. Very inexpensive lessons and rentals are available, but there is a small trail fee. During evenings you may ski on four miles of illuminated trails. Hayrides, showers, sauna, and camping facilities are at your disposal. Write: Blackhawk Ridge Recreation Area, Box 92-A, Sauk City, Wisconsin 53583. Telephone: (608) 643-3775.

Green Lake is operated as a conference center by the Baptist Assembly, but it's open to the public for a small trail fee. Seven hundred acres are reserved for cross-country skiing, with separate areas for snowmobiles and tobogganing. There are ten miles of marked trails through wooded terrain for all degrees of skill, from a one-miler to a 3¼-mile tour which has a hot chocolate rest station along the way. There are also fast downhill runs. Dawson House has a fireplace always in use and serves soup and chili. The whole complex, which includes five motels, is on Green Lake, 165 miles from Chicago, and all prices including rentals are reasonable. Write: Program Director, Green Lake Center, Green Lake, Wisconsin 54941. Telephone: (414) 294-3324.

Hardscrabble is 100 miles from the Twin Cities and has ten miles of trails through wooded terrain. Rentals are offered, and there is a trail fee; lodging is five miles distant. All comers are urged to bring their own lunches to cook, and even their own wine. The owner has no plans for expansion—he likes the place as it is—and doesn't want a bar. It's a place with a difference, indeed. Write: Hardscrabble, Rice Lake, Wisconsin 54868. Telephone: (715) 234-3412.

Snowcrest is a well-known school for the Professional Ski Instructors Association, and these same certified (Norwegian) teachers will take you in hand, too, for a moderate fee. There are nine miles of marked and maintained trails here, over half of which are lit for night touring. There is a trail fee and inexpensive rentals are available. During the week, ladies are encouraged by a good package plan to come for the day. An old farm house holds the rental equipment and sells hamburgers and soft drinks, but lodging is at Hudson House Inn, eight miles away. Or you can drive the 30 miles to the Twin Cities for everything. Write: Snowcrest, Route 1, Box 272-A, Somerset, Wisconsin 54025. Telephone: (715) 247-3852.

Telemark's trails were laid out by Sven Wiik, of Steamboat Springs fame, so you know this is no casual production. It has Sunday champagne brunches at the lodge and the chalet, at the base of the mountain, has drinking, dining, and dancing. The après-ski life is described as "plentiful." You can even ski on trails of carefully defined difficulty gradations. Instruction is available as are rentals, and there is a moderately steep trail fee. Three different ski-week packages are offered, and there is also Ladies' and Mens' Day during the week, with inviting price structures. You can stay at a townhouse which has everything and sleeps up to six, or at the lodge for more than you'd pay elsewhere. Write: Telemark Ski Area, Cable, Wisconsin 54821. Telephone: (715) 798-3811.

Whitecap has nine kilometers (not miles) of trails which are marked and maintained after each new snow. Both lessons and rentals are inexpensive, and there is a student package which no eligible person should overlook. Ask about family packages and the "super package." There is a game room, informal meals, and a ski repair shop, too. Write: Whitecap Mountains, Montreal, Wisconsin 54550. Telephone: (715) 561-2227.

THE WEST

California

Bear Valley Nordic Ski School is a resort high in the Sierra Nevada Mountains. It is surrounded by the Stanislaus National Forest and has all of 80 miles of scenic trails, all marked with the help of the forest service, and free for the use of the public. Instruction and rentals are available, and there are overnight touring trips to the cabin at Duck Lake. The more adventurous can bivouac in the snow. Shopping, formal dining, and entertainment are all here, and you will find various types of accommodations available. Write: Bear Valley Nordic Ski School, Box 96, Bear Valley, California 95223. Telephone: (209) 753-2325.

High Sierra Wilderness Guide Service escorts groups of up to six skiers or snowshoers on one- to ten-day adventures into the mountains. The cost is moderate, and there are family rates. They say that no experience is needed for snowshoers and just a minimum for skiers. Rentals can be arranged. Write: Guide Service, c/o Alpenhaus Ski & Mountaineering Shop, 2760 Fulton Avenue, Sacramento, California 95821. Telephone: (916) 483-9528.

Inyo National Forest has a fine free program for groups of 5 to 25 persons led by a ranger. Bring your own equipment (it's best if you aren't a rank beginner) and participate in tours arranged for holidays or Saturdays. This includes both ski-tourers and snowshoers. The forest service also provides free films, demonstrations about safety, slide presentations, and geology and wildlife gatherings. Write: Mammoth Ranger District, Box 146, Inyo National Forest, Mammoth Lakes, California 93546.

Kirkwood Meadows, although it does offer instruction for the novice, is particularly slanted to clinics for more advanced skiers and leans heavily toward racing on its 35 miles of marked (but not groomed) free trails. There is two-hour or full-day instruction available or a guided tour covering either five or 11 miles. Even a snow survival course with an overnight in a cave you have excavated for yourself, for the serious tourer. The center has limited accommodations, and lunches (but not rooms) are available from the Kirkwood Inn. Gear can be rented. Write: Kirkwood Meadows Ski Touring Center, Kirkwood, California 95646. Telephone: (209) 258-8864.

Lassen Park in northern California has touring snow until July, free, of course, to the public. At the southern entrance is Childs Meadows, which offers whatever you may need or want, including instruction, accommodations of various sorts, meals, gear rental and guided tours. Write: Childs Meadows/Resort, Mill Creek, California 96061. Telephone: (916) 595-2941.

Mammoth Cal-Nordic is another of the Californian hard-core places which has more to teach than you may want to learn. They offer the usual instruction, rentals, and tours, and in addition promote survival in the snow, cooking in drifts, avalanche advice, and mountaineering. There are even classes for the handicapped and blind. Use of the marked and maintained trails is free as is a map of the area. If you will not be spending the night in one of the institute's cabins or tents or in a snow cave, you may want to stay at Tamarack Lodge. Write: Mammoth Cal-Nordic Ski Touring Institute, Tamarack Lodge, Mammoth Lakes, California 93546.

Rock Creek Nordic is located between the John Muir Wilderness (to which it has unlimited access) and Route 395. Part of the lodging package is a snow-cat shuttle between the road and either the lodge or your woodfire-heated cabin (no plumbing). Free skiing is available in all of the wilderness and also on the ten miles of marked and maintained trails belonging to the lodge. There are lessons, lunches, and rentals (decreasing in price per day up to three days). In addition, there is guided mountaineering plus clinics on survival and safety in the winter mountains. Made-to-order tours to many possible destinations can be arranged, and there is a package plan. Write: Rock Creek Nordic, Box 404, Bishop, California 93514. Telephone: (714) 873-7349.

Royal Gorge offers everything up to and including a week-long trans-Sierra trip. It measures its trails in kilometers (50 of them), and the continental flavor includes the lodge which has dormitory sleeping arrangements, large fireplace, and a sauna. What's more, you reach it on skis. They offer guided tours, rentals, and instruction in addition to wilderness seminars. There are several packages, one of which is a trip to Donner Summit. Lodging is at the school or Soda Springs Hotel. Write: Royal Gorge Ski Touring School, Box 178, Soda Springs, California 95728. Telephone: (916) 426-3793.

Squaw Valley, on the edge of Lake Tahoe, offers the public free use of the 35 to 40 miles of marked and maintained trails used by Olympic cross-country skiers. There are lessons and rentals (reasonable) and a nice ski package including technique, overnights, and winter survival courses. Tours of every imaginable sort are offered as are group singalongs, wine and cheese parties, and ice skating. Write: Squaw Valley Nordic Ski Center, Box 2288, Olympic Valley, California 95730. Telephone: (916) 583-4316.

Tahoe-Donner Ski Bowl is the site each spring of the Far West Ski Association trip, which retraces the route of the ill-fated 1846 Donner Party. It is lead by ski-touring historians with a following of all interested parties. A network of 20 miles of maintained trails begins and ends at the lift area of this Alpine and Nordic center. There is no trail fee nor are there any rentals available. Instruction and tours, including overnights, are available as are midweek packages. Lodging is available at Tahoe-Donner Guest Ranch, Box 538, Truckee, California 95734. Telephone: (916) 587-2551.

Yosemite in winter is an experience every summer visitor ought to have (but not everyone at once). The national park has almost 90 miles of trails and roads for the public, plus shops, restaurants, and lodging either at Yosemite Lodge or the older, gracious Ahwahnee Hotel. The scenic areas and wildlife can be appreciated from many points, but think especially of the Dewey Point trail, which tops off at 7300 feet with a magnificent view of the valley and El Capitan. There is a mountaineering school with qualified instructors for all levels of competence, plus day and overnight tours and survival classes. Rentals are available as are midweek packages. The park service marks all trails and distributes maps free. The trails are of graduated degrees of difficulty. Write: Yosemite Park & Curry Co., Yosemite National Park, California 94389. Telephone: (209) 372-4611.

Colorado

Ashcroft is a ghost town, a wonderfully lonely area of cross-country trails amid the hussle and turbulence of the Aspen area. There are 24 miles of marked and maintained trails for which a trail fee is charged. The fee also entitles you to a hot drink at the huts found along the way. Rentals are available as are lessons. Many different sorts of tours are offered: all-day instruction, a dinner trip to Pine Creek Cook House, an overnight, or a two-dayer. Aspen, a half hour away, offers everything, including a free shuttle bus from the Hotel Jerome almost every morning. Write: Ashcroft Ski Touring, Box 1572, Aspen, Colorado 81611. Telephone: (303) 925-1971.

Breckenridge is a sophisticated place with, in addition to the Nordic skiing, downhill slopes, shops, restaurants, and a variety of lodging possibilities. Instruction is paramount here, and the three degrees of competence are separated to a greater extent than most other schools. Five miles of level and gentle slopes for the novice, 25 miles for the intermediate, and unlimited terrain, including some in deep powder, for the expert. Mountaineering courses are offered, and moonlight tours including tea and snacks are offered. Rentals are very reasonable. Write: Breckenridge Ski Touring School, Box 705, Breckenridge, Colorado 80424. Telephone: (303) 543-2368.

C & G Touring, at Fraser, has 3000 acres of territory with a network of trails for all. There is a fee for their use. The skier receives a tag, which when returned signifies he's back safe and sound. Lessons are offered for either full or half days, and gear rents for a small sum. Overnight and day tours are offered, there is a warming hut, and several packages can be arranged. Lodging is three miles distant. Write: C & G Touring Center, Box 174, Fraser, Colorado 80442. Telephone: (303) 726-5954.

Chuck Fothergill's isn't actually an area, it's a Nordic shop that gives lessons and guides excursions for skiers or snowshoers on over 200 miles of "informal" trails. Those close-in, however, become packed down with use. Rentals are available, and guided and moonlight tours are popular, especially with the visitor. The town of Aspen offers pre and post everything. Write: Chuck Fothergill's Outdoor Sportsman, Hunter & Cooper, Box 88, Aspen, Colorado 81611. Telephone: (303) 925-3288.

Copper Mountain Touring has 15 miles of beautifully marked and groomed trails broken down into three main loops of varying distances, plus a six-mile route which can be extended to eight, which goes to the base of Jacque Peak. All trails at this new area weave in and out of the timber line. Lessons are available, or you can participate in a half- or full-day tour to see evidences of the gold-mining period, lumbering days, and where sheep were tended a century ago. There is also a moonlight tour to an old cabin where you will stop for hot spiced wine and snacks. Write: Copper Mountain, Box 397, Frisco, Colorado 80443. Telephone: (303) 468-2882.

Crested Butte is for the ski-tourer who really wants to cover ground. The 50 to 60 kilometers of trails are marked but not maintained, and the enthusiastic skier can ski 25 miles over Pearl Pass and down into Aspen. Lessons and tours, which include a wine

In many areas it is possible to take along properly winterized recreational vehicles and use them as ski chalets. The necessary plug-ins and facilities are usually available.

and cheese lunch, are offered, and equipment rentals are available at the going rate. There are accommodations in all price ranges here. Write: Crested Butte Ski Area, Box 528, Crested Butte, Colorado 81224. Telephone: (303) 349-5326.

High Forest Inn is the place for you if you want low prices and a great variety of possible destinations. It is just at the edge of the Arapaho National Forest, which has 480 miles of trails for your enjoyment. Rentals are inexpensive as are the guided tours. The skier can tour the old town of Leadville and Dinosaur National Monument via bus, which leaves the Inn for one-day or overnight trips, or you can stay local and have the company of Maggie, the

St. Bernard who accompanies tourers "whether they like it or not." Either rooms or dormitory accommodations are provided. Write: High Forest Inn, P.O. Box 119-X, Hideaway Park, Colorado 80450. Telephone: (303) 726-9906.

Keystone, with its 10,000-foot altitude, continues to have good snow until Easter. Located in the Arapaho Forest, Keystone has a new web of trails in Montezuma Valley. Colorado's first discovery of silver was made at Montezuma, and you can reach this and other long-deserted mining towns on trails that are marked and maintained. There is no trail fee. Half- and full-day lessons are available as are rentals at reasonable rates. Consider a package plan and stay where you are, or find lodging at Dillon which you reach by shuttle bus. Write: Keystone, Box 38, Dillon, Colorado 80435. Telephone: (303) 468-2316.

Lake Eldora is a magnificent, wild place to ski, with some of the higher peaks of the Rockies towering above, heads often in the clouds. Pick up a USGS trail map in Boulder en route, as the trails are not patrolled and the weather is infamous for its sudden changes. Rocky Mountain wildlife is often encountered on the rugged trails. Rentals, lessons, and group guided tours are offered. There are no accommodations closer than Boulder, but a cafeteria and cocktail lounge are at the base lodge. Write: Lake Eldora Ski School, Box 438, Nederland, Colorado 80466. Telephone: (303) 447-8011.

Purgatory is certainly a misnomer for this beautiful ski-touring area near Durango in the San Juan Mountains. Lessons from top-notch instructors are available, and three tours, geared to competence, are offered. Overnights to cabins in the mountains are popular with larger groups (up to eight). Rentals are available, and there is a notable trail fee for use without lessons. All types and price ranges of accommodations are available with many different ski packages offered. Write: Purgatory Ski Area, Box 1311, Durango, Colorado 81301. Telephone: (303) 247-3838.

Rocky Mountain Expeditions are not to be undertaken lightly, but for the competent, hardy adventurer who wants a true mountain snow experience, a rugged trip for from one to five days into the Continental Divide area would be perfect. Expect trips into the back country, perhaps to Mt. Elbert, Colorado's highest peak, where cabins or Arctic expedition tents are used. The trips include guides, shelter, food, and equipment and can be tailored to your needs. Read Chapter 11 in this book before embarking. Write: Rocky Mountain Expeditions, Inc., P.O. Box 576, Buena Vista, Colorado 81211. Telephone: (303) 395-8466.

Scandinavian Lodge, Steamboat, is THE area in Colorado. You go there for any purpose from seeing the lodge with its shop, sauna, and gym, to receiving basic instruction. There are clinics on everything from "selection and care of equipment" to getting into the business yourself to racing camp. High-quality equipment can be rented, and there is no trail fee. Write: Scandinavian Lodge, Box 5040, Steamboat Village, Colorado 80499.

Vail is the OTHER place in Colorado. Best known for Alpine skiing, the cross-country program is also large, with 145 miles of unmarked trails extending beyond the golf course instruction area. Much of the terrain is difficult going, and it is recommended you go with a guide. There is a night tour where all participants wear lights on their heads and stop for a hot snack en route. Rentals are higher priced than usual as are lessons. Vail, a self-contained community, has countless available accommodations, a large number of ski packages, restaurants, and shops in superabundance. Write: Ski Touring School, Box G., Avon, Colorado 81620. Telephone: (303) 476-3116.

Idaho

Craters of the Moon offers just a few more facilities for visitors than our astronauts found on their lunar expedition. The area is unique with its strange depressions, caves, and solidified lava flows. There are campgrounds, but no electricity. Fires may be built in fireplaces but only with wood which has been brought in by the camper. The town of Arco is eighteen miles away, and here arrangements for overnights may be made and rental gear is available. Here, also, are the closest food supplies. For the hardy, Craters is an unforgettable experience. Write: Superintendent, Craters of the Moon National Monument, P.O. Box 29, Arco, Idaho 83213. Telephone: (203) 527-3257.

Sun Valley probably has more ways to ski than any other. Consider night-touring to a cabin for a wonderful dinner, or a day-long bus trip for a small group plus guide with stops en route for scenic ski-tours. Probably the most unusual is a helicopter trip into the backcountry where you may ski the wilderness in solitude or with a group and be picked up at the end of the day. Or ski out and fly back. There are 100 miles of marked and maintained trails free to the public, and the lesson packages are unlimited in scope and variety. Sun Valley has everything for the skier, from a private condominium to bowling lanes. Write: Sun Valley, Sun Valley, Idaho 83353. Telephone: (208) 622-4111.

Montana

The Big Mountain, just south of Glacier National Park, has 20 miles of trails plus "at random" skiing. Just a small portion is marked and groomed. There are inexpensive rentals and half-day instruction. Lodging is available at several places locally. Write: Big Mountain Ski Shop, Box 683, Whitefish, Montana 59937. Telephone: (406) 862-3511.

Big Sky, in the Spanish Peaks Primitive Area, has superb scenery and 35 miles of trails from which to appreciate it. There is no trail fee, but the steep rental price more than makes up for that. Instruction is at the going rate. One-day guided trips are offered, and lodging can be found right there at hostels or condominiums. Write: Big Sky of Montana, Box 1, Big Sky, Montana 59716. Telephone: (406) 995-4211.

Bridger Bowl has fine dry snow plus good scenic views of the Bridger Range. There are 15 kilometers of trails, plus open skiing. Rentals and instruction, very moderately priced, originate at the chalet. There is an attractive five-day package. Everything else available 16 miles away at Bozeman, Montana 59815. Telephone: (406) 586-2787.

Glacier National Park does have high-country skiing, and if you are a very skilled skier and will go with several others of like competence, you might like to tackle this area, avalanche danger, or no. Consult with park rangers before any excursion into the wilds. Most people will be far happier on the lower ground around Lake McDonald. There are no rentals, no food, and no lodging at Glacier, but the prepared may wish to camp here. Write: Glacier

National Park Headquarters, West Glacier, Montana 59936. Telephone: (406) 888-5441.

Montana Snow Bowl offers 18 miles of trails, rentals, and modestly priced all-day instruction. Nila Lodge holds 60 people in various sorts of accommodations and also has ski packages. There are overnights and day tours. The lower of the two lodges provides food, the upper hut serves to warm you at the top. Write: Montana Snow Bowl, Box 1164, Missoula, Montana. Telephone: (406) 549-9006.

Nevada

Slide Mountain/Mt. Rose is just 22 miles from the jet-port in Reno or is easily reached by driving on Interstate 80. There are only 5 kms of marked and maintained trails for the ski-tourer here, but the beautiful views of the mountains, Lake Tahoe, and the Nevada desert make up for it. Typical of so many low-latitude, high-altitude ski areas, the snow is dry powder. Use of the trails is free and instruction is available at very moderate rates. Write: Slide Mountain/Mt. Rose, Box 2406, Reno, Nevada 89505. Telephone: (702) 849-0704.

Oregon

Hoodoo Ski Bowl is a place out of the ordinary in that the main skiing done is Alpine touring, done on heavier mountaineering equipment. Hoodoo is just adjacent to the Pacific Crest Trail, and the experience of skiing this is different and exhilarating for the skilled and adventurous. Most of the local skiing is done on forest service land between Mt. Washington and Mt. Jefferson so there is no charge for use of the trails. At this time Hoodoo gives lessons only through the University of Oregon, but they do rent equipment at a modest fee. Nearest accommodations are at Black Butte Ranch, ten miles distant. Write: Hoodoo Ski Bowl, Camp Sherman, Oregon 97730. Telephone: (503) 595-6678.

Mt. Bachelor is located just at the border of the Three Sisters Wilderness Area and has only a ¾-mile novice track of its own.

Those with more experience venture across Dutchman's Flat to the forest service trails in the wilderness. There is no check-in or-out system or patrolling, so the prudent skier is advised to make his own arrangements. There are rentals, and rather expensive instruction is available. Accommodations of all types are available at nearby Bend. Write: Mt. Bachelor, Box 828, Bend, Oregon 97701. Telephone: (503) 382-2442.

Mt. Hood Region, with its forest service roads which are unplowed and unsnowmobiled during the winter, offers miles of free scenic touring. They are not maintained, nor is there a check-in/out system, so skiers are advised to travel in groups and carry emergency supplies. The ranger station at the Zig-Zag on the route to Mt. Hood has maps you should get. A good overnight tour is 2-C, which begins at Still Creek Road entrance and goes upward for some miles before dropping down to Kinzel Lake. There is a lean-to here to provide shelter. The most traveled is 1-A, which starts at Still Creek Road and Highway 26. It's 4½ miles across open land and then a circle of Trilium Lake for an easy, pleasant trip. Write: U.S. Forest Service, Region 6, P.O. Box 3623, Portland, Oregon 97208.

Utah

Brighton Ski Bowl is part of the new Park City ski area about 30 miles east of Salt Lake City. Park City is geared mainly to Alpine skiers, and Brighton's 17 miles of trails are not well marked, nor are they patrolled. A heavy snow falling on light powder means avalanche conditions, so advising someone of your trail and expected time of return is a wise course. Mt. Majestic is the lodge you may choose. Instruction and rentals are offered at reasonable rates. Write: Brighton Ski Bowl, Brighton, Utah 84121.

Bryce Canyon National Park, with its steep trails and sharp turns into the canyons, is for the experienced skier, although there are short trails for the beginner on the rim drive. There are 70 miles of trails in all, and that's a lot—especially when they are free to use. The park offers no lessons or rentals, and there are no lodging facilities in the boundaries either. Within ten miles of the perimeter, however, there are at least three places to stay—that is if you don't get permission and overnight in Bryce itself. Write: Superintendent, Bryce Canyon National Park, Bryce Canyon, Utah 84717.

Cedar Breaks National Monument is in southwest Utah, on terrain less tortured than Bryce, and has miles of good trails for the cross-country skier, affording fine views of the Badlands. Dixie National Forest is close by, and although it has no trails as such, the terrain is good and even the road from Cedar Breaks to the forest which is not plowed during the winter makes a good path. Brianhead Ski Resort, a few miles distant, or Cedar City, 20 miles away, have lodging. Write: Superintendent, Cedar Breaks Nat'l Monument, 491 S. Main, Cedar City, Utah 84720.

Park City Resort is a large, booming ski area with condominiums, restaurants, bars, shops, lifts for Alpine skiers, and 50 miles of trails for the ski tourer. Add to this its proximity to the old mining town with century-old sagging clapboard buildings and wooden sidewalks, and you have an area to hold your interest when the muscles fail. Trips into the mountains can be arranged through Wolfe's Ski Shop which also has instructors available and supplies for winter camping. Park City is 30 miles from Salt Lake City. Write: Wolfe's Cross-Country Shop, Park City Touring Center, Box 27, Park City, Utah 84060. Telephone: (801) 521-2131.

Park West is just three miles from Park City, and its guides can take you on a cross-country trip on old mining trails from claim to deserted claim. See the Old West on skis. You can rent equipment if need be. Write: Nordic Ski Touring Co., Box 348, Park City, Utah 84060. Telephone: (801) 649-8594.

Powder Mountain is a rather new area 50 miles northeast of Salt Lake City, seventeen miles from Ogden. It now has 20 miles of maintained trails for the ski-tourer. Overnights are a specialty here, and there are the usual rentals and instruction available. Lodging is at condominiums which are close by. Write: Powder Mountain, Box 117, Eden, Utah 84310. Telephone: (801) 745-3771.

Snow Basin is also near Ogden, which is where the nearest accommodations are. There are only eight miles of groomed trails at Snow Basin, but rentals and group lessons are very low-cost. Write: Snow Basin, E. Miller Ski School, 1657 24th Street, Ogden, Utah 84401.

Snowbird has perhaps the lowest-cost rental/instruction package anywhere for either a half or whole day. It also divides itself into three areas for the various degrees of expertise of the skier. For the tourer in his first season and the intermediate there is Little Cottonwood Canyon; for the more skillfull skier there are Red and White Pine Canyons; and for the advanced person, the extension of Cottonwood Canyon. A variety of lodging options are offered. Write: Information Director, Snowbird Corp., Snowbird, Utah 84070. Telephone: (801) 742-2222.

Snowland Ski Area is where you want to go if you hate the Park City atmosphere of everything for everyone. Snowland is in the center of the state and is the least developed area in the West. No lodging (nearest is eight miles away in Fairview), no rentals, and no instruction. Just you and the powder snow. Right there in the Manti-LaSal National Forest. Follow the 32-mile trail and listen to the silence. Write: Snowland, Fairview Canyon, Fairview, Utah 84629.

Zion National Park (Lava Point Area) is open during the winter, and the hard core cross-country skier may just love it. The road is open, but often only four-wheel-drive vehicles can negotiate the route. The scenery, as at all of Utah's parks, is spectacular, and more so under a blanket of snow. No facilities await the skier, so bring your own and plan to overnight in either Hurricane or Springdale, just a few miles from the boundary on Route 15. Write: Superintendent, Zion National Park, Springdale, Utah 84767. Telephone: (801) 772-3221.

Washington

Cascade Corrals offers adventure for intermediate and advanced skiers, for whom there are one- to three-day backpack trips with guides. For even more off-beat activity there are helicopter rides which fly gear into high-country shelters. You ski this new area for the bulk of the day, then tour out to the highway by evening. All equipment is provided: sleeping gear, shelters, packs, snowshoes, etc. Beginners receive instruction and winter camping in the Cascade Mountains. Rates depend entirely on arrangements. Write: Cascade Corrals, Stehekin, Washington 98852.

49° North happens not to be near the North Pole at all, but just an hour's drive north of Spokane. Lessons are inexpensive, equipment rental high, so it averages out. There are 30 miles of trails here through a wooded area and an additional 30-acre area for free skiing, so you shouldn't be running into too many others. Packages are offered, and accommodations are ten miles away at Chewelah. Write: 49° North Ski School, Box 166, Chewelah, Washington 99109. Telephone: (509) 935-6649.

Mission Ridge has 15 miles (three trails) plus more tracks for ad-lib skiing. Rental price depends on just what is hired and lesson rates depend on the size of the group. Overnights and packages can be arranged. Lodging is 12 miles from the area in Wenatchee. Write: Mission Ridge, Box 1765, Wenatchee, Washington 98801. Telephone: (509) 663-7631.

Northwest Alpine Guide Service offers classes in waxing, technique, and snow terrain, plus day lessons and group excursions. Touring weekends along the deepest glacier-carved canyon in Washington, Icicle Creek, are favorites with no more than 18 participants permitted. Sleeping is in tents with insulated floors. Before the opening date in December, free lectures on touring are given at the Seattle and King County libraries. Write: Northwest Alpine Guide Service, P.O. Box 80345, Seattle, Washington 98108. Telephone: (206) 762-5165.

Wyoming

Grand Targhee Resort, north of Jackson Hole and south of Yellowstone National Park, is reached through Driggs, Idaho and has good powder snow until April, with cover of some sort remaining until June. Half- and full-day instruction is available, and gear rental is inexpensive. There are lots of marked trails, but only about seven miles of them are maintained. Overnights and packages are available, and there is a wide range of types and prices of accommodations at Grand Targhee. A base lodge, open throughout the day, has a restaurant and lounge. Write: Grand Targhee Resort, Alta, Wyoming, via Driggs, Idaho 83422. Telephone: (307) 353-2308.

Grand Teton National Park has seen a population explosion in recent years of cross-country skiers, from 157 tourers in 1965 to well over 4,000 last year, and it is little wonder, with the grandest peaks in the country within a dozen miles of Jackson. All

Heated ten-passenger snow cruisers take skiers and snowshoers from West Yellowstone, Gardiner, and Jackson Hole to the winter wonderland around Old Faithful.

the hiking trails used so extensively during the summer are available, sketchily marked and not maintained, but beautiful and free to all. Guides and equipment, if needed, are available in Jackson or at Teton Village (see below). For maps and information, write park headquarters. One trail begins at the Whitegrass Ranger Station, climbs to 7200 feet to overlook Phelps Lake, and then leads into Death Canyon. Another winds its way up Signal Mountain from the Lodge for a spectacular view of the valley (or "Hole") and both of these and others offer matchless beauty. Sudden, harsh storms arise quite often, so the wise skier enters the area prepared for the worst. All provisions, lodging, and gasoline must come from Jackson. Write: Grand Teton Park Headquarters, Box 67, Moose, Wyoming 83012. Telephone: (307) 733-2880.

The Jack Pine, in Jackson, is a shop which offers ski-touring instruction and rentals. Where you go and for how long is individually determined according to skill and preference. The prices depend on your choices. Tours may go to the Pot Hole area, Teton Pass, with its splendid scenery, or into Grand Teton National Park to the Bradley-Taggart Lake region on a trail usually packed by previous skiers. Write: The Jack Pine, Box 1904, Jackson, Wyoming 83001. Telephone: (307) 733-3699.

Powderhound tours are run within Grand Teton National Park from a base at Teton Village, the mecca for downhill skiers. The scenery is unsurpassed, the trails only roughly marked, and it's make-your-own or follow the route of earlier tourers. There are full- and half-day lessons with or without gear rental. Overnights and week or weekend packages are available, and lodging is available at the many accommodations in Teton Village. Write: Powderhound Ski Tours, Box 752, Jackson, Wyoming 83001. Telephone: (307) 733-2208.

Snow King is the town of Jackson's answer to Teton Village, both of which cater mainly to Alpine skiers. Snow King also has cross-country instruction, and rentals at moderate rates and package specials can be arranged. Touring is in many of the nearby scenic areas in various sorts of countryside. Cache Creek, Grand Teton National Park, and Leeks Canyon all have a vast skiing area of unmarked trails which are not maintained. Accommodation is at the Alphorn Lodge, directly across the street from the downhill ski area in town. Write: Snow King Cross Country, Box R, Jackson, Wyoming 83001. Telephone: (307) 733-2851.

Sundance Ski Tours, in this same magnificent area, offers half- and full-day tours and rentals of high-quality equipment at a moderate cost. Along with instruction and the tour, "an awareness and respect for the delicacy of the various ecosystems in the area" is instilled. Overnights and extended tours can be custom-made to fit interests, needs, and experience. All winter camping equipment is available with the exception of personal clothing. Write: Sundance Ski Tours, Box 1226, Jackson, Wyoming 83001. Telephone: (307) 733-4449. Or stop in at Jackson Hole Ski & Sports store

At one time skis furnished the only way to get around the Tetons in winter. Now more modern skis make touring a tremendously rewarding sport.

on the north side of the town square. Sundance also has an office in Teton Village at the base of the mountains.

Yellowstone National Park is to many people even more beautiful in winter than during the summer—and certainly host to only a fraction the number of guests. The blue, yellow, and green thermal pools dot the snow-covered landscape, the geysers rumble and bubble and erupt as they always do, but during the winter the circling evergreens become upholstered with layer upon layer of frost, snow, and glitter. Elk, buffalo, moose, and deer are subdued; their only concern is survival through the bitter Rocky Mountain winter. From just before Christmas to mid-March, Snow Lodge at Old Faithful is open, with its plain rooms, crackling fireplace, and cafeteria-style meals. Snowshoes and cross-country ski equipment can be hired at a rate above costs at more ordinary areas. Instruction is available as are ranger-guided tours among the wonders of the park. A six-day Ski-Tour'er package is available starting either in Bozeman, Montana, or Jackson, Wyoming, which includes meals, lodging, and touring the most outstanding features in the park with knowledgeable guides. For the experienced skier, there is The Nordic Package, a five-day, four-night tour into a remote

Old Faithful in Yellowstone is never more thrilling, more spectacular than when viewed after a ski or snowshoe tour from Snow Lodge.

area with a dependable guide to lead you. This is a truly memorable winter experience. The Nordic tours begin every week, from early January to early March. Bring your own proper clothing and a sleeping bag to keep you warm to 30 below zero.

The one discordant note here is that snowmobilers are welcomed and are in noisy evidence, especially over weekends. There are even meets here during the winter. Imagine hundreds of roaring internal combustion engines at one time. Avoid these dates at all costs. Write: Yellowstone Park Company, Yellowstone National Park, Wyoming 82190. Telephone: (307) 344-7311.

THE SOUTHWEST

New Mexico

Angel Fire doesn't sound like an area with snow, but indeed it does fall (and stick) here at Eagle Nest, close to the Colorado border.

Several years ago the area was purchased by a large corporation which to date has pumped $5.5 million into the 22,600-acre resort. There are marked and maintained cross-country trails plus large areas where open skiing can be had. Accommodations, of course, are right here at any one of three facilities. Write: Angel Fire, Eagle Nest, N.M. 87718. Telephone: (505) 377-2205.

Bandelier National Monument, near Los Alamos, has spectacular scenery and even a herd of deer. However, the area is one of cliffs and very steep inclines, and it is no place for the beginner to begin. For the experienced skier, however, touring the canyons is exhilarating. All touring must be done on established trails. Write: Superintendent, Bandelier National Monument, Los Alamos, New Mexico 87544. Telephone: (505) 672-3861.

Taos, with its southern latitude combined with high elevation, has a very light powder snow. Although it caters mainly to downhill skiers, there are eight miles of marked and maintained tracks for the Nordic skier. Lessons, rentals, and packages are available. Full- or half-day tours go to Kachina Peak or the Wheeler Wilderness. All facilities are found in the valley. Write: Taos Ski Valley, Inc., Taos Ski Valley, New Mexico 87571. Telephone: (505) 776-2266.

Trail Adventures De Chama are headquarters for any group of skiers who want a guided tour, winter camping, or even racing for up to a week in New Mexico's most scenic area. The trips are individually tailored to the skiers' abilities and desires. Up to ten persons are taken with two instructors or guides; food and lodging provided. Write: Trail Adventures De Chama, 5839 Idlewilde Lane S.E., Albuquerque, New Mexico 87108.

ALASKA

Alyeska is the place where skiers, both Alpine and cross-country, come from Anchorage and all other global points for racing and pleasure skiing. Alaskan rates for almost everything are far higher than those found elsewhere in the U.S., but the cost of lessons and rentals here are just about the same as those in the "lower 48." There are loops from the 10-kilometer racing track, or try touring the frozen Glacier Creek in the wooded lower areas of the mountain. If neither suits, just ski at will on the large meadow. There is no charge for this or the use of the trails. Stay at the Nugget Inn. Write: Alyeska Resort Inc., Box 578, Girdwood, Alaska 99587. Telephone: (907) 783-4232.

Denali Dog Tours and Wilderness Freighters operates mainly in McKinley Park using "the north's most historic, adventurous, and aesthetically pleasing modes of wilderness transportation"— dog sleds. The teams, possibly with skiers and snowshoers, accompany cross-country ski-tourers or ski-mountaineers who want to travel long distances, but without heavy, encumbering backpacks. Often old patrol trails are followed and nights are spent in original ranger patrol cabins or heated tent camps. There are real challenges here, and you will be a participant in meeting them, not an observer. Stamina and coordination are essential. You will need to provide your own suitable clothing and sleeping gear (and it could reach 50° below), so bring your own or rent them from the booking agent, Eberhard's, in Anchorage. For transportation and other information write Eberhard's Sport Shop, 307 E. Northern Lights and Denali, Anchorage, Alaska 99755.

Genet Expeditions offers snowshoeing or ski-touring trips for groups of one to four or five or more for three to ten days in Mt. McKinley Park country. Learn some climbing and glacier training while there. You fly one way or round trip with a bush pilot to Ruth Glacier Amphitheatre at the base of Mt. McKinley, or to Pirate Lake. Some degree of coordination and expertise is necessary for a trek where you'll see bear, moose, Dall sheep, and caribou. Write: Genet Expeditions, Talkeetna, Alaska 99676. Telephone: (907) 733-2606.

Nordic Ski Clubs maintains marked trails in Chugach State Park which wind above and below the timber line. You can ski these thirty miles and/or take a three-lesson instruction package for a nominal fee. Write: Nordic Ski Club of Fairbanks, Box 5-111, College, Alaska 99701.

14

Where to Go: Canada

Alberta

Banff Park has over 60 miles of trails, marked and maintained by rangers. Their use is free, and the surroundings are a justly world-famous scenic area.

Lake Louise in Banff Park, rents equipment and gives instruction. The Skoki Lodge is open to skiers for several months each year. Extensive tourist facilities offer everything. Write: Lake Louise Ski Area, P.O. Box 5, Lake Louise, Alberta.

Marmot Basin, 11 miles from Jasper, connects with Jasper Park's 800 miles of trails and offers high bowl skiing and marathon runs from 8557-foot Marmot Peak. Write: Marmot Basin Ski School, Box 472, Jasper, Alberta.

Mount Norquay, three miles from Banff, has a "challenge" mountain plus Wishbone Trail area where less-than-expert skiers can tour.

Sunshine Village, also in the Banff area, has excellent bowl skiing on fine snow. The trails are its own or the park's. Look into a springtime tour toward Mt. Assiniboine. All trails lead to Sunshine Lodge, P.O. Box 1510, Banff, Alberta.

British Columbia

Apex-Alpine, in the Okanagan Valley, has much of the dry, fluffy, and fast snow for which the area is known. The emphasis here is on steep, tricky trails for skilled skiers, although there are some for the less confident. It's located 22 miles from Penticton on Green Mountain Road. Write: Apex-Alpine Resort, Penticton, British Columbia.

Big White concentrates on the intermediate-caliber skier, with long, gradual wide trails sloping down from an open-faced top. It shares the Okanagan Valley with Apex. Write: Big White, Route 33, Kelowna, British Columbia.

Burke Mountain is an inexpensive area to ski and not far from Vancouver. It offers 35 to 40 miles of trail. Write: Burke Mountain, 2693 West Broadway, Vancouver, British Columbia.

Cross-Country City offers inexpensive rentals and instruction on 40 miles of trail. Lodging is at nearby Prince George. Write: Cross-Country City, 2693 West Broadway, Vancouver, British Columbia.

Gibson Pass is a popular family area 145 miles from Vancouver on H-P Highway in Manning Provincial Park. Rentals, lessons, and 200 miles of trail are available. Manning Park Lodge, Gibson Pass, H-P Highway, British Columbia.

Grouse Mountain is a five-minute ride via the Grouse Mountain Skyride from the North Vancouver terminal to the top third of the big monolith. Ski night or day. Accommodations at Grouse Nest, Grouse Mountain, North Vancouver, British Columbia.

Kimberley Ski Area, just 50 miles from the U.S. border, has 17 miles of groomed trails and many types of accommodations from which to choose. Write: Kimberley Ski Area, Kimberley, British Columbia.

Red Mountain is really a two-mountain complex (Red and Granite), either one a skier's delight. Just two hours' drive from Spokane, it offers skiing for all but concentrates on big tests for experts. Write: Red Shutter Inn, Rossland, British Columbia.

Silver Star has four miles of marked trails adjacent to another 25 miles of blazed but not maintained trails in Silver Star Provincial Park. A family area with rentals and instruction available, it features a Winter Carnival in February. Silver Star is fourteen miles from Vernon. Write: Silver Star Ski Area, 2813 30th Street, Vernon, British Columbia.

Whistler Mountain, 75 miles north of Vancouver, is the giant among North American slopes, with a 4280-foot vertical from deep

Canadian resorts usually have ample facilities and room for both snowshoeing and cross-country skiing.

powder bowls at the top to an evergreen base. Experts desiring solitude can take a helicopter to nearby glaciers and carve turns in unmarked virgin-powder snow. Write: Whistler Mountain, Garibaldi Park, British Columbia.

Manitoba

Manitoba has four cross-country ski areas, but these do not operate every day or all day during the week, so check with Director of Manitoba Tourism, Winnipeg, Manitoba, Canada R3B 2E7 before your trip.

Tows operate all day every day (December to April) at Holiday Mountain at *La Riviere*, 107 miles southwest of Winnipeg. *Falcon Lake* in Manitoba's Whiteshell Provincial Park, 96 miles east of Winnipeg, offers all winter sports for the tourist, and skiing is good at *Mt. Agissiz* in Riding Mountain National Park near Mc-Creary and *Mt. Glenorkley* near Brandon. Both have overnight accommodations for the holiday weekender.

New Brunswick

There are 11 ski areas currently operating in New Brunswick ranging up to the 800-foot vertical at *Poley Mountain* near Sussex. Many areas operate in the afternoon with night skiing through the week, switching to full days on weekends and holidays.

Top runs are found at *Crabbe Mountain* (700 vertical), 40 miles from Fredericton, *Mount Douglas* (750 vertical), on Highway 7, 45 miles north of St. John, and *Mount Farlange* (600 vertical), at Edmundston.

The northern New Brunswick snow belt includes *Mount Kodiak* (400 vertical), at Campbellton in *Sugarloaf Provincial Park*. Noted for consistent snow conditions and well-groomed trails, Sugarloaf is a solid weekend bet, with good accommodations nearby in town.

Newfoundland

Thanks to the fine art of conversation, which Newfoundlanders maintain at a high standard, a visitor rarely remains a stranger for very long in *Corner Brook*. *Marble Mountain* (550-foot vertical drop), just eight miles from *Corner Brook*, features runs ranging from easy to steep. *Smokey Mountain* (1,000 vertical) is a remote but well-equipped ski area at Labrador City in the Iron Mountains of Labrador. Accessible either via Eastern Provincial Airlines or Quebecair out of Montreal, the club boasts a complete range of lodge facilities and services in addition to a ski season that extends into June.

Nova Scotia

Forty-five miles northwest of Truro is *Wentworth Hostel* and just beyond are 35 miles of cross-country trail. They are not maintained, and there is no fee for their use. Very low-cost lessons and rentals are available through the Canadian Youth Hostel Association which accepts donations toward the purchase of trail-setting equipment. Write: Canadian Youth Hostels Association, Maritime Region, P.O. Box 3010 South Halifax, Nova Scotia.

Ontario

Blue Mountain offers good touring over open-land skiing including Bruce Trail, running high on a ridge overlooking Georgian Bay. Instruction and rentals are high for Canada, about what you'd pay in the U.S. Write: Blue Mountain Park, R.R. 3, Collingwood, Ontario.

Echo Ridge offers free touring over 25 kilometers of trail which are groomed now and then. This is also a country club. It offers lessons, rentals, overnights, and ski packages. Write: CSIA, The Cross-Country Dept., Echo Ridge, Box 137, Kearney, Ontario.

Georgian Peaks is crowded with Toronto skiers on weekends but during the week has lots of room. It boasts the highest vertical and some of the best runs in Ontario.

Hidden Valley is in the heart of the Muskoka resort area. Although not a particularly high mountain, the extensive ski terrain favors the novice but also interests the intermediate. No trail fee; everything else runs average U.S. rates. Write: Hidden Valley Highlands Ski Club, R.R. 2, Group Box 74, Huntsville, Ontario.

Horseshoe Valley has 11 miles of groomed trails over what is a golf course during the summer. The runs are short and the atmosphere is convivial. Write: Horseshoe Valley Resort, Box 607, Barrie, Ontario.

Limberlost includes a lodge and rustic cabins with fireplaces deep in the wilderness at the edge of Algonquin Park. It has over 135 kilometers of trails, all marked and maintained. Weekend trips to a cabin and a midweek package are also offered. Sleigh rides, ice skating, and saunas are available. Prices high but not outrageous. Write: Limberlost Lodge, Box 1560, Huntsville, Ontario.

Loch Lomond's trails course down both sides of a valley, and the area's 800-foot vertical distance offers a wide choice of terrain, including twin slopes, "Jolly Giant" and "Giant Slalom," on the north face complex. Write: Loch Lomond, Highway 61, Thunder Bay, Ontario.

Mt. McKay's Big Chief area, just recently opened, now rates as the largest ski development in Thunder Country. The new trails add a degree of challenge to McKay, previously regarded as a top intermediate class area. You'll find McKay just three miles south of the international airport. Write: Mt. McKay, Highway 61B, Thunder Bay, Ontario.

Mt. Norquay is a little picture area with a 750-foot drop comprised of three major runs and seven subsidiary trails. Although not a large area, it certainly has some of the best skiing in the Thunder Bay area, including Thunder Bowl run. Write: Mt. Norquay, Highway 61, Thunder Bay, Ontario.

Oktoberfest is a truly remarkable place 48 miles north of Toronto, just south of Barrie. Here, on 70 acres, you will find cross-country trails, snowshoe/nature trails, and an ice skating rink flood-lit for evening use. All these facilities are free, and you may even use the equipment at no cost. Bring your own ice skates, but there are more than 200 sets of cross-country equipment and 50 pairs of snowshoes for your enjoyment. The Keg Inn has hot snacks at nominal cost, and the Barrel House, a 4800-square-foot "après-ski lounge," is available for special occasions. All this courtesy the Octoberfest Cross Country Ski Centre, Formosa Springs Brewery, Barrie, Ontario.

Talisman is a complete ski resort area with wide-open runs and a good range of trails for both the novice and advanced skier. It is 90 miles northeast of Toronto. Write Talisman Resort Hotel, Kimberley, Ontario.

Quebec

Eastern Quebec is divided into two areas, eastern townships and Quebec City. The eastern townships are in a natural snowbelt with

Ski-touring in Canada—what better way to get away from it all?

the longest seasons in eastern Canada. They lie just north of the U.S. border and are composed of six major areas all easily accessible via the Eastern Township's Autoroute, southeast of Montreal. The areas are *Owl's Head, Glen Mountain, Mont Sutton, Bromont, Mont Orford,* and *Mont Echo,* and all are close enough to each other that a single ticket is offered, allowing the guest to ski each area from one base of operations.

Quebec City has three bustling ski areas within minutes of downtown.

Mont-Ste.-Anne is 27 miles east of the city. The recent development of the north side of this 2000-foot peak has nearly doubled the choice of terrain and has extended the season into late spring. Day lodges are available at both the summit and base. *Lac Beauport* is the traditional vacation area located 15 miles north of the city in a sheltered valley. The lodges and manors nestled at the base are proud of their French cuisine. *Stoneham* has a network of 10 well laid out trails and is located 19 miles from Quebec City. There is a large day lodge at the base area and, in addition, there are scheduled bus services to nearby resorts and to the city itself.

Western Quebec is also divided into two major areas, the Laurentian Mountain region and an area of the national capital.

Less than an hour's drive north of Montreal, in the Laurentian Mountains, is the most highly developed year-round resort area in Canada. Here is the heaviest concentration of ski hills of any area of similar size in the world. The entire sector is accessible by the Laurentian Autoroute.

St. Sauveur-des-Monts, 40 miles from Montreal, marks the start of the 40-square-mile Laurentian ski complex that extends north to Mont Tremblant. Included here are *Piedmont, Mont-Gabriel, St.-Adele, Ste.-Marguerite, Val-Tremblant, Chateau Montebello,* and *Far Hills.*

Within an area ranging from 12 to 60 miles from the capitol, Ottawa, are six major ski developments. Five, (*Camp Fortune, Vorlage, Edelweiss Valley, Mont Cascade,* and *Mont Ste.-Marie*), are all in Quebec and all within commuting distance of the city via Highway 11. The sixth, *Calabogie Peaks*, is also in this area but happens to be across the border in the province of Ontario. All the pleasures of city life are available in Ottawa.

The provincial government of Quebec maintains countless miles of ski-trail networks at *Laurentides Park, Mont-Ste.-Anne-Park, Mont Oreford Park* and also at *Duchesnay Forestry Station.* They also operate tours. These are worth exploring. Write: Director General of Tourism for Quebec, Canada, 17 West 50th Street, New York, New York 10020.

Bibliography

BOOKS ON SKIING AND SNOWSHOEING

Bauer, Erwin A., *Hunting with a Camera*, New York, Winchester Press, 1974

Brunner, Hans & Kälin, Alois, *Cross-country Skiing*, trans. by Wolfgang E. Ruck, Toronto, McGraw-Hill Ryerson Limited, 1972

Caldwell, John, *New Cross-Country Ski Book*, Brattleboro, Vermont, The Stephen Greene Press, 1971

Kjellstrom, Bjorn, *Be Expert With Map and Compass*, New York, Charles Scribner's Sons, 1972

Lederer, William J. & Wilson, Joe Pete, *Complete Cross-Country Skiing & Touring*, New York, W. W. Norton & Co., 1970

Osgood, William & Hurley, Leslie, *The Snowshoe Book*, Brattleboro, Vermont, The Stephen Greene Press, 1972

Riviere, Bill, *Backcountry Camping*, New York, Doubleday & Co., 1971

LOCAL AREA TRAIL GUIDES

Ski Touring Guide to New England. Medora Bass, ed.; 2nd ed. 1973, published by Eastern Mountain Sports, Boston, Massachusetts; 286 pages in a 3-ring binder, $4.50. Lists trails and areas in Connecticut, Massachusetts, Vermont, New Hampshire, and Maine.

Ski Touring Guide. Ski Touring Council; 1973–74 ed., published by Ski Touring Council, Troy, Vermont; 92-page booklet; $2. Primarily trails and areas in Vermont and New York State, with a few in other East Coast states.

Ski Tours in California. David Beck, Far West Ski Association; 1972, $4.95. Some advice on touring plus descriptions of 38 tours in Sierras, some ski mountaineering routes.

Ski Minnesota, A Cross-Country Skier's Guide to Minnesota and Western Wisconsin. Gary Noren and Dwight Olsen; published by the authors in cooperation with the North Star Ski Club, 1973; 95-page, 8½ x 11-inch, spiral-bound stenciled, $2.75. Lists 77 areas, with maps for most.

A Guide to Ski Touring Covering Colorado, Southern Wyoming and New Mexico. Morgan Queal, ed.; published by the Rocky Mountain Division, United States Ski Association, first edition 1972; 54-page booklet, $2. Lists trails in major ski areas and national parks along with quadrangle map information.

Washington Nordic Tours. Brad Bradley; published by Signpost, 16812 36th Avenue W., Lynnwood, Washington 98036, $3.95.

Aspen Tourskiing & Cross Country. Raymond N. Auger; published by Columbine Books, Box 2841, Aspen, Colorado 81611; 59-page booklet, 1971, $1.75.

Cross-Country Skiing in Toronto and Southern Ontario. Annabel Slaight, ed.; published by Toronto Life, 56 The Esplanade, Toronto, Ontario, 1974; 63-page booklet, $1.95.

Winter Adventures, Ontario, Canada. Booklet published by the Ministry of Industry and Tourism, Government of Ontario, Parliament Buildings, Toronto, Canada M7A 1T3. Contains a chapter on cross-country ski areas.

Cross-Country Ski Trails in the Laurentians. Map published by LaZone de Ski Laurentienne, 300 Place d'Youville, Montreal 125, Quebec, 1971; $1.50.

FOR INFORMATION ON SKI-TOURING AREAS IN SPECIFIC STATES

California: Far West Ski Association, 812 Howard Street, San Francisco, California 94103. The FWSA publishes a "Ski Touring Annual" every year listing events, clubs, and where you can find instruction, lodging, huts.

Colorado: Holubar Mountain Ltd., Box 7, Boulder, Colo. Also: U.S. Forest Service, Building 85, Denver Federal Center, Denver, Colorado 80225.

Maine: State of Maine Publicity Bureau, 929 Gateway Circle, Portland, Maine 04102

Michigan: Southeast Michigan Travel and Tourism Association, Executive Plaza, 1200 6th, M-150, Detroit, Michigan 58226.

Montana: Advertising Unit, Room 53, Montana Highway Department, Helena, Montana 59601. Also: U.S. Forest Service (Northern Region), Federal Building, Missoula, Montana 59801.

New Hampshire: Division of Economic Development, P.O. Box 856, Concord, New Hampshire 03301.

New York: State Department of Environmental Conservation, Albany, New York 12202, or State Office of Parks and Recreation, Albany, New York 12223. Also: Ski Touring Council, 51-01 39th Avenue, Long Island City, New York 11104 for their "Ski Touring Guide" ($2.25).

Oregon/Washington: Northwest Alpine Guide Service, Inc., P.O. Box 80345, Seattle, Washington 98108. Also: U.S. Forest Service, Region 6, P.O. Box 3623, Portland, Oregon 97208.

Wisconsin: Wisconsin Department of Natural Resources, Bureau of Commercial Recreation, Box 450, Madison, Wisconsin 53701 for the brochure/locator guide, "Wisconsin Ski Touring Opportunities."

Ontario: Ministry of Industry and Tourism, Travel Service Branch, Hearst Block, 900 Bay Street, Toronto, Ontario. (Ask for the booklet, "Ontario Winter Adventures.")

General Information: The Ski Touring Council (West Hill Road, Troy, Vermont 05868) publishes a "Ski Touring Guide" ($2) and an annual "Schedule" ($2.50) outlining ski-touring activity in New York, New Jersey, Pennsylvania, and New England. The Appalachian Mountain Club (5 Joy Street, Boston, Massachusetts 02108) also has information on touring in Massachusetts, Rhode Island, Maine, and New Hampshire.

Index

Algonquin Indians, 21
Athapascan Indians, 21
Automobiles, cold weather and, 129–
30
Avalanches, 141–47

Biathlon, 22
Bindings
  ski, 32–33
  snowshoe, 38–39
Boots, 25
  skiing, 30–33, 46–47
  for snowshoeing, 38, 46–47

Camping, winter, 89–101
Canadian sites, 197–204
Carson, Charlie, 96–97
Catlin, George, 20–21
Clothing, 43–53
  boots, 46–47
  gloves, 49
  goggles, 51–52
  hats, 47–49
  lightweight shell jacket, 46
  pants, 44–45
  shirts, 44
  socks, 44
  sunglasses, 49–51
  sweaters, 45
  underwear, 43–44
  vests, 45–46
Coarse-grained snow, 72
Coggeshall, Almy, 68–69

Cold weather, coping with, 136–38
Compass, 84, 135
Cross, C. Joseph, 63
Cross-country trails, 77–87
Cross member, 36–38

Emergencies and accidents, 129–39
Equipment, 25–41
  boots, 30–33
  poles, 33–34
  skis, 25–30
  snowshoes, 34–41
  waxing kits, 30
Exposure, 136–37

Fiberglass, 25
Fine-grained snow, 72
First-aid, 86–87
  emergencies and, 129–39
Fishing, 115–26
Flambeau, Pete, 126
Foods, high energy, 134–35
Freeze dried foods, 94
Frostbite, 86

Gaiters, 46–47
Gloves, 49
Goggles, 51–52

Hats, 47–49
Heat loss, 132–34
Herringbone, 70

History of cross-country skiing, 19–23
Hunt, Sir John, 39
Hunting, 115–26
Hypothermia, 137

Igloo building, 90, 98–99
Indian use of snowshoes, 20–21

Jackets, lightweight shell, 46

Laying trails, 79–81
Length, ski and pole, 28
Light-touring skis, 27–30
Locations and sites
    Canadian, 197–204
    U.S., 149–95

Maps, 84, 135

Neoprene, 34–36, 41
New snow, 72
Nighttime ski-touring, 81–84

Origins of cross-country skiing, 19–23
Overnighting, 89–101

Pants, 44–45
Photography, 103–13
Physical fitness, 60–63
Poles, 25
    ski, 28, 33–34, 70–72
    snowshoeing, 41, 58–59
Prater, Bill and Barbara, 39–41

Racing skis, 27–30
Rucksacks, 25, 41, 94–95
Running waxes, 72

Sherpa snowshoes, 39–41
Shirts, 44
Side step, 70
"Ski Touring Guide," 67
Ski-touring techniques, 65–75
Skiing, 25–34
    beginning technique, 65–75
    origins of, 19–20, 22–23
Skis, 25–30
Sleeping bags, 94–95
Snowmobiles, 79

Snowplowing, 70
Snowshoeing, 34–41
    beginning technique of, 55–63
    origins of, 19–22
Snowshoes, 34–41
Socks, 44
Sportsman's Eye, The (Gregg), 53
Stick waxes, 72
Storm kit, 86–87
Stoves, 92–94
Sunglasses, 49–51
Survival kits, 86
Sweaters, 45
Switchback, 60, 70
Swix, 72

Technique
    beginning snowshoeing, 55–63
    ski-touring, 65–75
Temperature and weather, 138–39
Tents, 90–92
Tinned waxes, 72
Touring skis, 27–30
Tracks, 106–107
Trails, cross-country, 77–87
    laying, 79–81
Traversing, 60
Tube waxes, 72
Tuque, 48–49
Turning, 60

Underwear, 43–44
U.S. sites, 149–95

Vests, 46–47

Waist carriers, 25, 41
Warm-up pants, 46
Warren, Tom, 141
Waxing, 72–75
Waxing kit, 25, 30
Weather, 107
Webbing, 34–36
Whitefishing, 116–20
Wildlife watching, 103–13
Wind and temperature, 138–39
Winter camping, 89–101
    sleeping bags for, 94–95
    stoves for, 92–94
    tents for, 90–92